Editor
Lorin Klistoff, M.A.

Managing Editors
Karen Goldfluss, M.S. Ed.
Elizabeth Morris, Ph.D.

Editor-in-Chief
Sharon Coan, M.S. Ed.

Cover Artist
Barb Lorseyedi

Art Manager
Kevin Barnes

Art Director
CJae Froshay

Imaging
Rosa C. See

Product Manager
Phil Garcia

Publisher
Mary D. Smith, M.S. Ed.

GRAPHIC ORGANIZERS
Grades 4–8

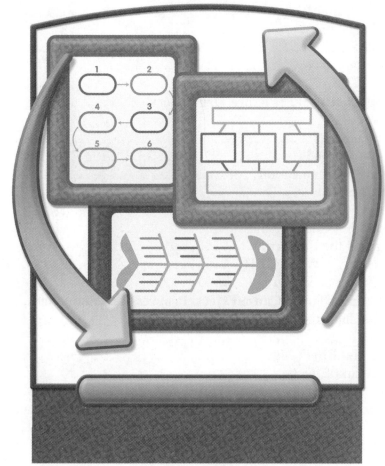

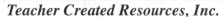

Author
Casey Null Petersen

Teacher Created Resources, Inc.
6421 Industry Way
Westminster, CA 92683
www.teachercreated.com
ISBN-0-7439-3208-0
©2004 Teacher Created Resources, Inc.
Reprinted, 2005
Made in U.S.A.

Table of Contents

Table of Contents

Introduction

We all use graphic organizers of some kind, and to some degree, every day of our lives. A menu, a train schedule, a calendar, and even a guide to television programs are all examples of graphic organizers. They are beneficial in making it possible for us to visualize information in a condensed and organized form. They also make it possible for us to organize plans, thoughts, and ideas. They help writers to organize thoughts before writing. They are the tools that help us to learn, process information, envision, and create.

If students become familiar with graphic organizers at an early age, they are more likely to have an understanding of how to organize ideas and concepts, how to think more clearly, how to plan with a goal in mind, and how to relate concepts, ideas, and facts to other concepts, ideas and facts. Learners, of all kinds, are better able to visualize information and ideas when familiar with graphic organizers. They are better able to access information, understand information, and organize and present information.

There are a variety of graphic organizers included in this book and a variety of ways to use them. The organizers are arranged according to their types and similarities, but many graphic organizers may be used for multi-purposes. Any graphic organizer may be modified (expanded, simplified, or combined) to suit student capabilities, the intended purposes of the organizer, or an entirely new use. The organizers may be reproduced, copied after being modified, used individually, in groups, or enlarged for whole-class use.

Each section begins with an introduction offering suggestions for the uses of its graphic organizers. In addition, the simpler organizers are nearer the beginning of each section progressing to the more complex toward the end. Nevertheless, the graphic organizers in this book can be modified so that they are suitable to younger and older students. Some suggestions for ways to do this are found in the introductions.

Some organizers come with filled-in examples to get started, but that does not mean that the organizer can only be used in that manner and with that kind of subject matter. Some organizers come with very little direction, in part because they may be such common organizers that their usage is well known and they are included so that they may be readily accessible, and in part because some organizers are open-ended enough that your own interpretation, and the interpretations of the students, is encouraged.

Creativity is also encouraged. With familiarity with the organizers in this book, it is hoped that students and teachers will feel competent in creating new, useful, and specific organizers for their own needs. Learning is often fluid and organic, and so, organizers to facilitate such processes ought to also be organic and fluid. Graphic organizers can be created on the fly, as it were, while in process and in need of a way to structure what is being created, imagined, or analyzed.

Some kinds of organizers appear more than once in the book, with different purposes in mind. Even then, the uses of graphic organizers are not limited to only those purposes, and perhaps could be placed in every section of the book with some modification.

This book offers only a few of the many graphic organizers available. In addition, there are those that you are inspired to create after having experience with these. Each graphic organizer can be modified, combined, and/or revised to fit the needs of students and the lessons being prepared. While there is some overlap between the books, for graphic organizers more suitable for younger students, see TCM #3207, *Graphic Organizers Grades K–3*.

Spinning Webs

This section begins with the *Brainstorming Rules* (page 6) because students of all ages need to be reminded that brainstorming is a time to withhold judgment and let the ideas flow. *Brainstorming Web* (page 7) follows. This graphic organizer can be used while brainstorming, for recording ideas as a result of brainstorming, or for individual brainstorming. The best brainstorming is done as a group, however, and so it is recommended that the web be written on a chalkboard or white board to facilitate whole-class brainstorming whenever possible. *Web Questions* (page 8) is a graphic organizer that can be useful at more than one level. In the circle, the student writes a question he or she has pondered. It could be a question generated from reading, from a unit of study, or a research question. On the lines radiating outward from the circle, students can record their predictions about the answer, where they will look to find the answer, or related information and questions. In the box at the bottom of the page, they can record the answer. If this web is used on a regular basis, it could be stored in a notebook so that students will have a collection of questions answered and the work that went into finding the answers.

Clustering is an important skill for organizing thoughts and concepts. It's useful for research, note-taking, and prewriting, among other things. An example of a cluster can be found on page 9, and a blank cluster (page 11) for student use. Keep in mind, however, that clustering is often a free-form kind of activity with bubbles coming off at seemingly random locations. If clustering is used for a research paper, for instance, it is likely to be less free form, and more even-handed. When clustering is used as a prewriting activity for creative writing, a paragraph, a poem, to develop a character, a vignette, etc., it is more likely to take on a free form and even random organization. Encourage students to experience clustering in many forms including a pre-set amount of bubbles, more like a structured web to be filled in, and as a structure that grows freely in the moment, along with their thoughts and ideas. Because clustering is more of a process than a graphic organizer to be filled in, a clustering activity is included on page 10. Students should have many opportunities to practice clustering in different ways, especially to generate ideas for writing.

A *Vocabulary Web* can be found on page 12. It might be useful to have each student keep a notebook of his or her filled-in copies of this web. It will be his or her own personal dictionary. The information is available at a glance when it is organized this way, making it easier for students to expand and retain their vocabularies. The *Prefix Webs* activity on page 13 will strengthen vocabulary skills as well as understanding of word relationships. Use the blank one (page 14) that follows to create additional prefix webs and suffix webs. Other word webs might include word roots, synonyms, homonyms, etc.

Brainstorming Rules

How to Brainstorm

1. Write down every thought and idea. Every thought and idea has value.

2. Record thoughts and ideas very quickly. Keep things moving with a rapid flow of ideas.

3. Do not interrupt the flow to judge any thoughts or ideas. Record all thoughts even if they seem off topic, unrelated, or even dumb.

4. Remember that ideas that do not seem worth recording might prove to be important after all. At the very least, they may lead to other valuable ideas.

5. Brainstorming can be done alone, but the more people involved in the process, the more ideas will be generated.

6. Keep brainstorming until the ideas slow down. Take a deep breath, pause, and be ready to record some more ideas. They will still trickle in for a while.

7. When the ideas finally seem to slow to a stop, look over what was generated.

8. Use the best ideas.

6

Brainstorming Web

Directions: Write a word in each circle that tells about or describes the topic.

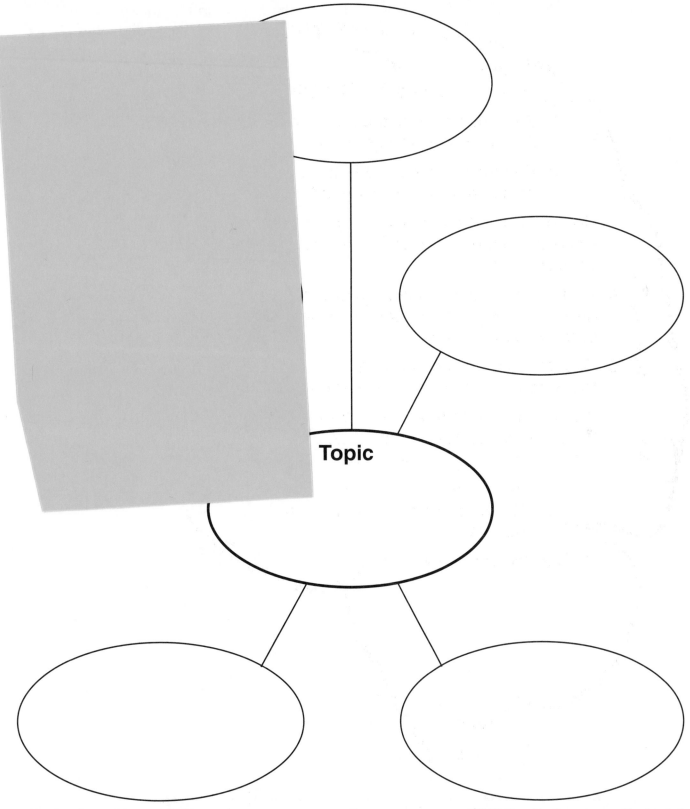

Topic

Web Questions

Directions: In the circle, write one important question. On the lines coming out of the circle, write information that relates to the question. Then, in the box, write the answer to the question.

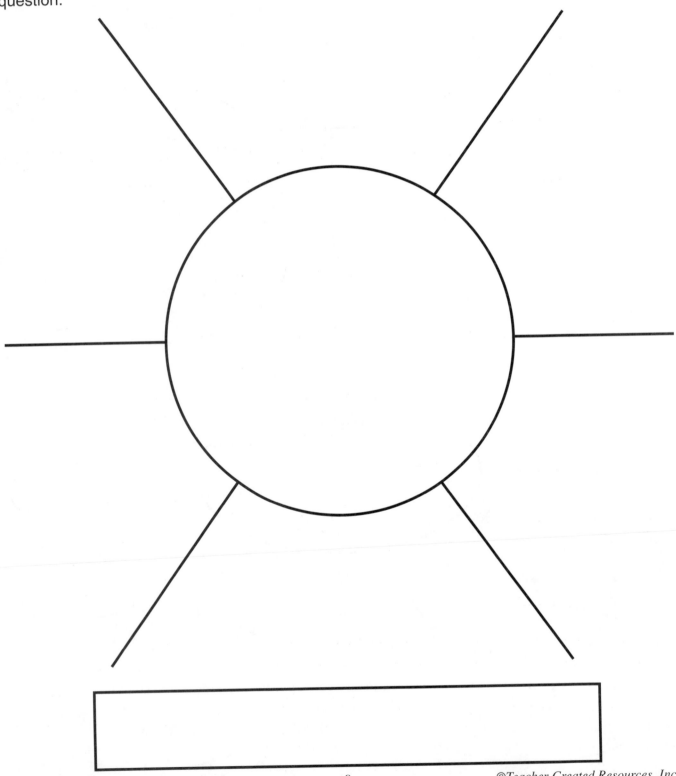

Clustering

Here is an example of how one student clustered her ideas about the mountains and the paragraph she wrote when she was finished with her cluster. You can use this as a model and an example as you learn how to cluster.

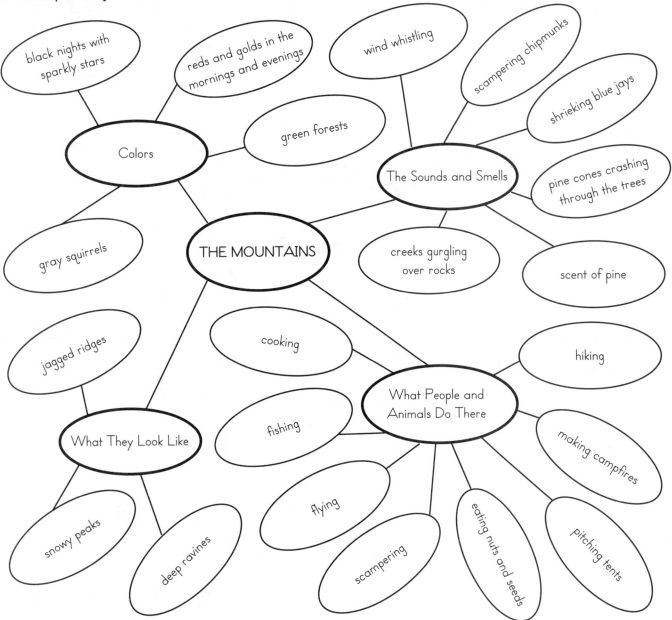

I love the smell of the dark, green forests and the campfire. These are smells that tell me I will soon hear scampering squirrels and gurgling creeks. As we pitch our tents, I see chipmunks and shrieking blue jays crunching on nuts and seeds. I know that soon we'll catch some fish and cook them while the wind whistles through the pine needles. Then we will hike to the top of a jagged ridge, look into many deep ravines, and watch the red and gold sunset turn into black sky, twinkling with endless, sparkly stars. I love the mountains!

Clustering

Using the cluster example on page 9, cluster your ideas related to the four seasons below. When you have finished, write a poem or paragraph about your favorite season, or about all of them.

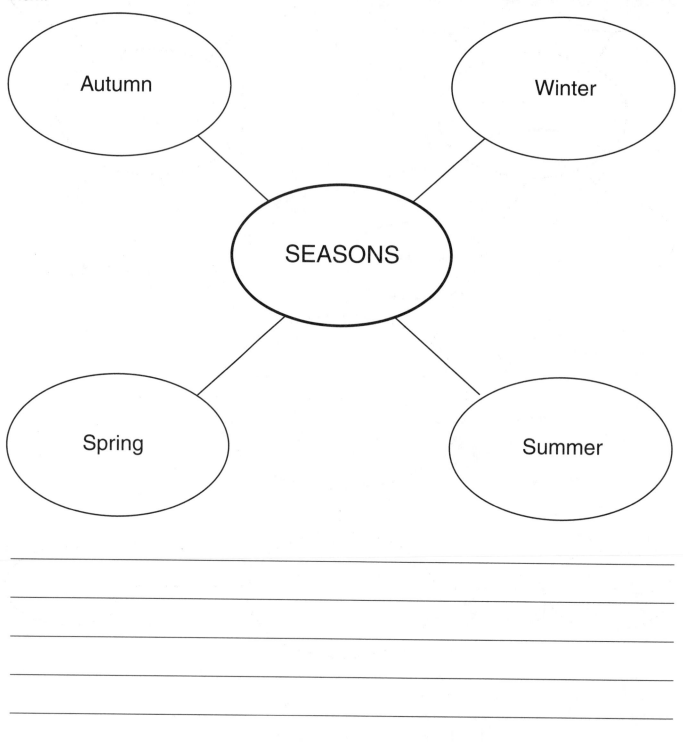

_____

_____

_____

_____

_____

_____

Clustering

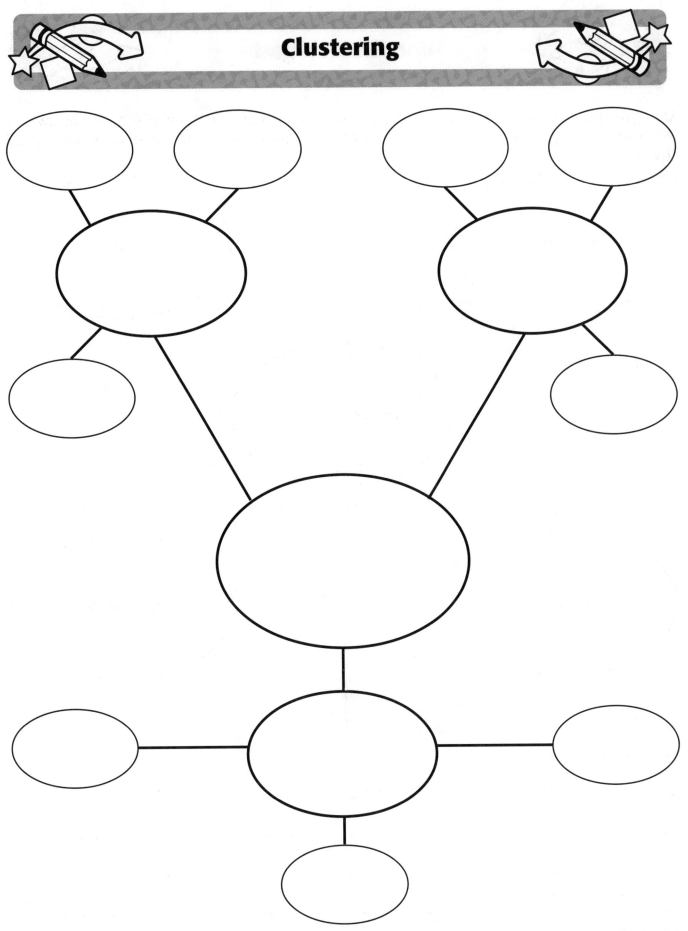

Vocabulary Web

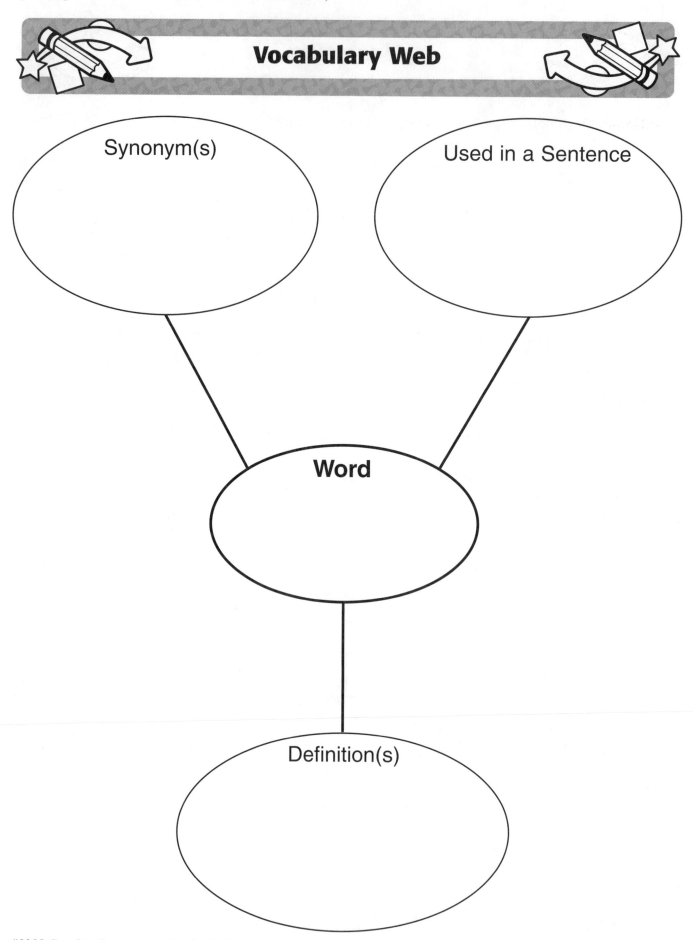

Synonym(s)

Used in a Sentence

Word

Definition(s)

Prefix Webs

Directions: Complete each web with other words that include the prefix.

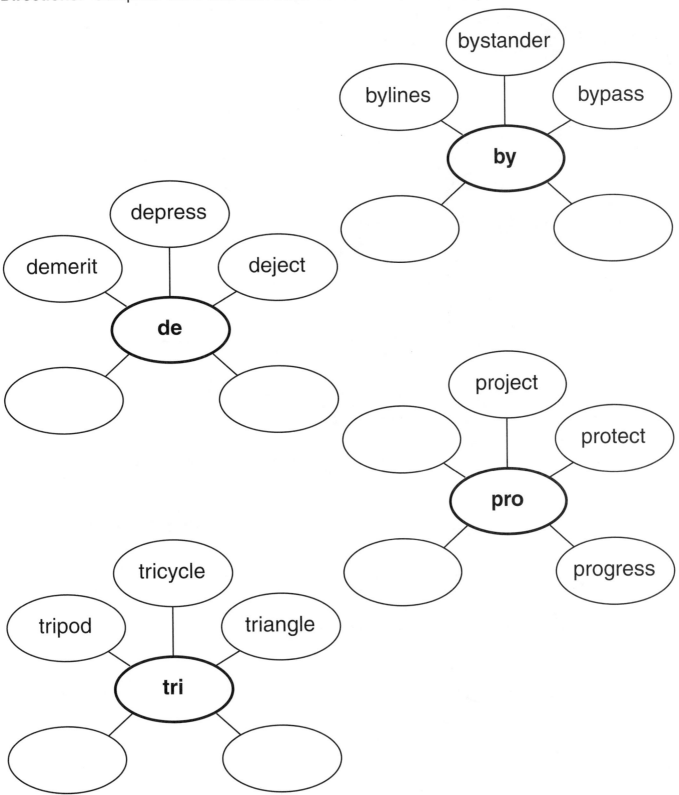

Prefix Webs

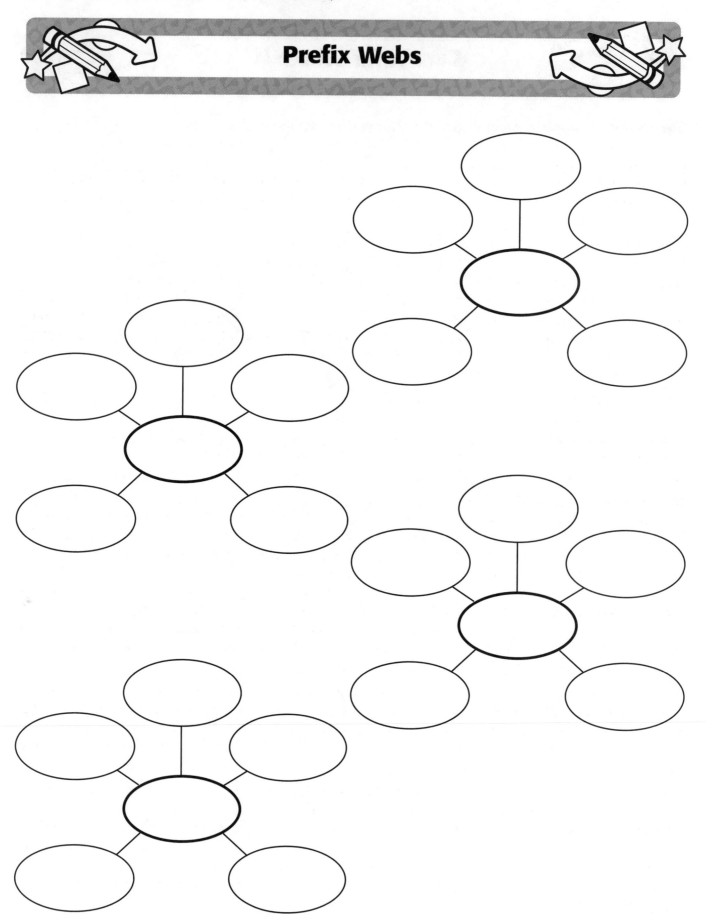

Can You Picture It?

This section on picture organizers begins with a graphic organizer, *What I Saw* (page 16), to allow students to record the pictures in their minds. Read to them, and then have them draw what they "saw." Discuss the different interpretations. Use this organizer for other subjects as well. For instance, students can draw scenes from history, as they visualize them. The organizer can also be used for book reports, when students draw favorite scenes and then prepare written or oral reports to accompany their television scenes.

The picture organizer, *Be Somebody!* (page 17), has many uses. It can be used as a template for filling in information about a fictional or historical character. Students can write about themselves in the shape. The figure can be divided up into parts as a graphic organizer for character analysis. For instance, the head portion could be used to talk about what the character thinks, the heart/chest area, what the character feels, the arms and legs, what the character does. Brief essays could be written on the form with the head being the main point, the body being the body of the essay, hands as supporting points, and feet as the conclusion. The figure may also be useful for health and science topics, or even for self-portraits to post along the walls.

Similarly, *The Open Mind* (page 18) is a picture organizer that has many uses. In addition to recording a character's thoughts, it can be used to write a narrative, as if the thoughts of an historical figure. Students might also record their own thoughts on a particular topic, for a class book. Again, the organizer is even useful for self-portraits, especially at the beginning of the year.

While *A Map to Organization* (page 19) is designed for prewriting, it can also be used to analyze a book or story. Encourage students to use this graph as an example or idea and to create their own picture map organizers. The *Tree Organizer*, found on page 20, has endless uses. It can be used, of course, for student family trees, as well as for the families of historical and fictional figures. It can also be used to organize information with the trunk being the main idea and the branches and roots being subtopics and details. The roots can represent causes and the branches, effects. Students may wish to use the tree organizer for clustering, brainstorming, or webbing, with the topic written on the trunk and ideas and thoughts arranged amongst the branches and/or roots. On page 21, there is a *Horse Organizer* that will help visual students organize their thoughts. They can each write their main idea on the mane, and the body of their support or details on the body of the horse. Have them keep their horses on their desks as they write their paragraphs or essays.

Make Me a Cheese Sandwich (page 22) will provide students with a memorable and unique way to organize their thoughts. You may want to reinforce the concept of the main idea and details by talking about how the top of a sandwich bun is the topic and the lettuce, tomatoes, cheese, and condiments (details) are what make it delicious. If you make a sandwich while instructing students, you will really get their attention.

Weighing the Choices, on page 23, is a graphic organizer that can be used in several ways. It can be used as a prewriting exercise for a comparison and contrast or opinion essay. It can be used for problem solving or debate. Or, given a topic, students can use the organizer for analysis. This section concludes with helping hands. Pages 24 and 25 offer two hand graphics. The first is *The Handy 5 Ws and 1 H*. Have students use it for writing paragraphs, preparing presentations, and for research and interview questions. For older students, use the *Five-Sentence Paragraph* hand for organizing their paragraphs. Have them write their ideas on the hand, in order, and their essays can follow the format. More capable students can use the organizer for a five-paragraph essay.

What I Saw

Directions: Draw the picture in your mind.

Be Somebody!

Can You Picture It? (Picture Organizers)

The Open Mind

A Map to Organization

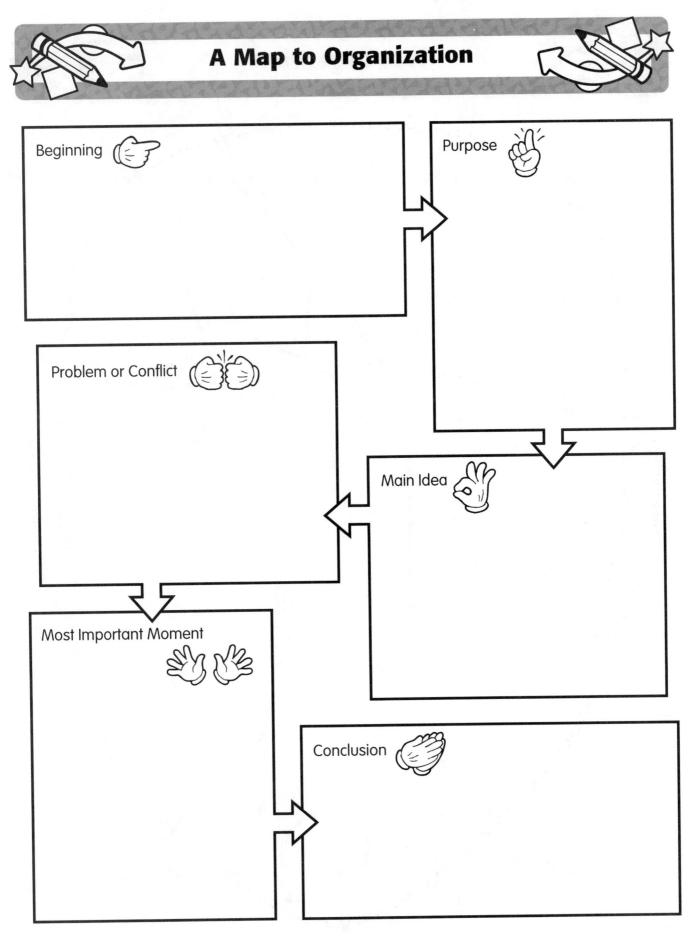

Beginning

Purpose

Problem or Conflict

Main Idea

Most Important Moment

Conclusion

Tree Organizer

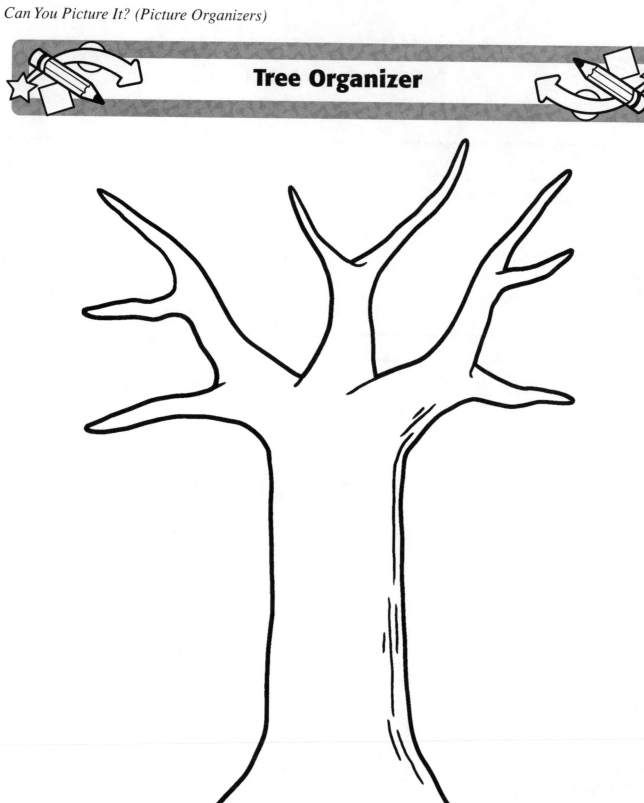

Horse Organizer

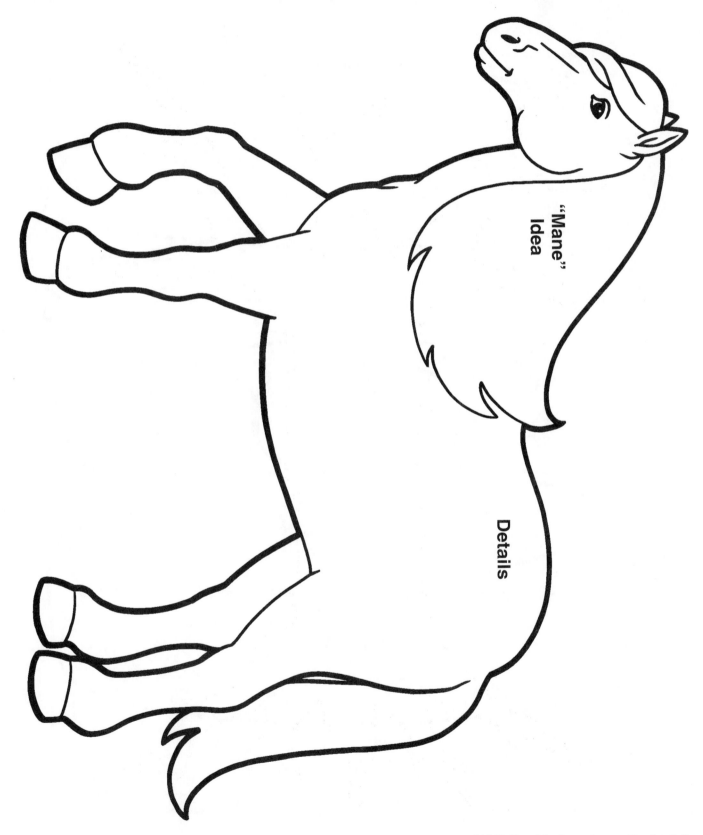

"Mane" Idea

Details

Make Me a Cheese Sandwich

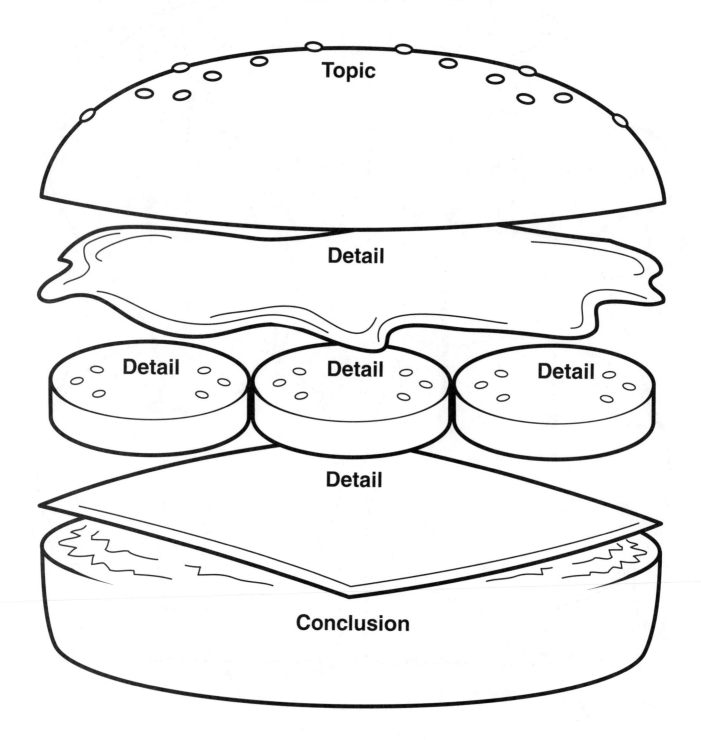

Topic

Detail

Detail   Detail   Detail

Detail

Conclusion

Weighing the Choices

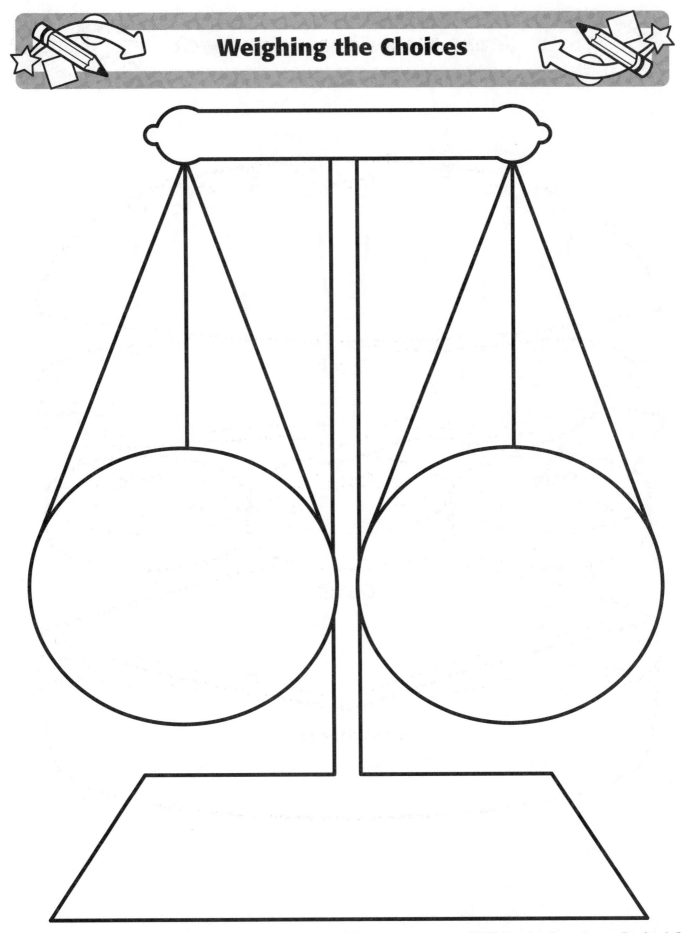

The Handy 5 Ws and 1 H

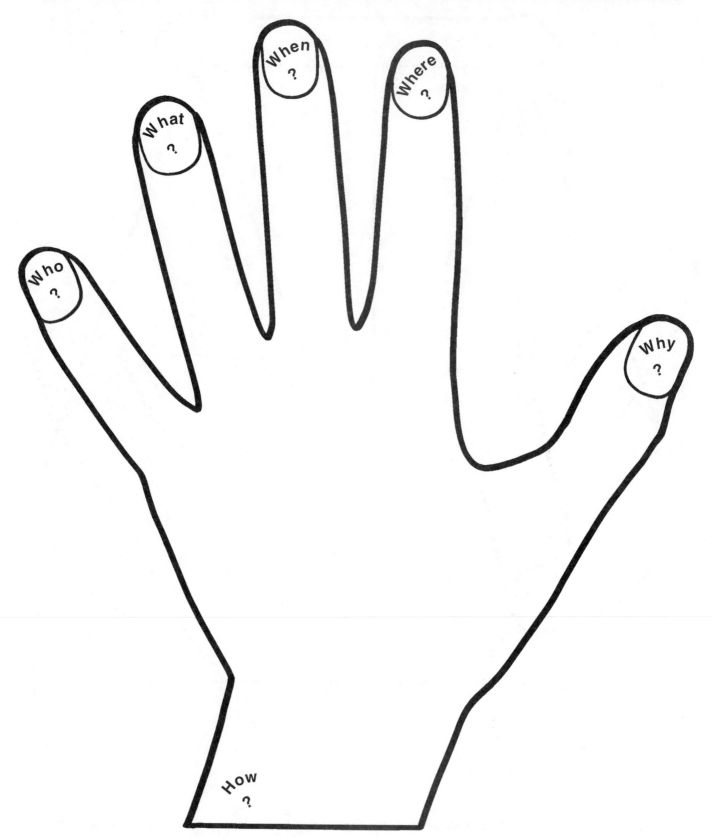

Five-Sentence Paragraph

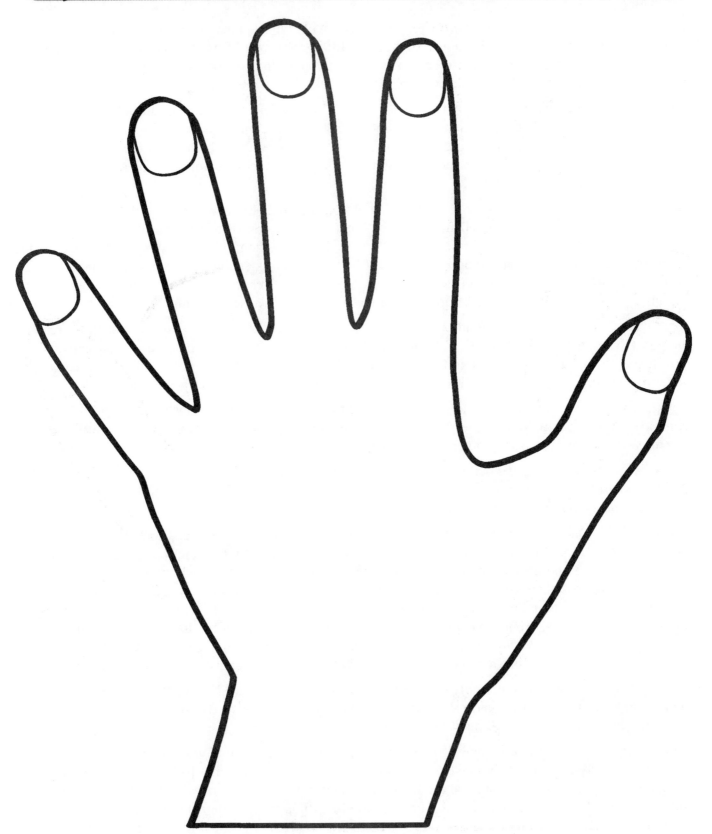

One Step at a Time

This section begins with *Causal Chains* (page 27) which will help students to be able to visualize sequences in cause and effect. For practice, they can fill in their own ideas, or give younger learners some brainstormed causes such as "the baby was climbing out of the crib" or "the elevators were broken," etc. Single chains can be photocopied and enlarged to make handy graphic organizers whenever needed.

The *Fishbone* organizer on page 28 will additionally enable students to see how multiple causes can lead to an effect. This fishbone organizer is unlabeled in order to be more versatile in use. Students may, for instance, write an effect (The Cold War, Uniforms at School, etc.) on the head of the fish and list the causes on the little bones. Students can also graph the main idea, a conclusion, and the details in an organized fashion under subtopics.

On page 29, there is a *Cause and Effect Map*. While it has many uses, an especially effective use would be for prewriting. Have students fill in the boxes with the cause and effects. Instruct them to consider transitional words and phrases such as "therefore," "and then," etc. They can write these along the arrows. *Causes and Effects* (page 30) is useful for many causes and many effects, with one topic, such as a period in history. Instruct students to ask themselves, "What happened?" when filling in the Effects column, and "What made it happen?" when filling in the Causes column.

What Would Happen If . . . ? is found on page 31. The question, "What If?" is one that inspires creative thought (Example: "What if we had four arms and hands?"). The organizer may be used to generate story ideas, story endings, or to more fully develop a character (published or not). Questions can be generated about history, social studies, etc. ("What if Pearl Harbor had never been bombed?").

Causes and events can be like dominoes, one causing the next to fall. A demonstration of falling dominoes might be a good object lesson, and a tie-in to studying world events in history as well. *Herringbone* (page 32) visually depicts the falling dominoes look in a pattern.

Time Line on page 33 is generically useful for history, autobiographical information, and various events. Use it to chart the growth of seedlings, drawing their appearance in the boxes and adding the dates below, as one example of another way to use a time line.

Ideas in Order (page 34) is a useful form that students can use anytime they need to get their points or steps in order. Have them fill in the form before demonstrating how to do something, arguing a point, or writing an opinion paper. Use the form as prewriting for an essay, and check their organizers before they write to be sure they have a clear idea about what they want to say and how they want to say it. The same concept is found in the *Ideas Map* (page 35), which gives more of a visual view of the process, similar to a storyboard. Some students may want to draw in the boxes of the Ideas Map to help them remember a sequence. *Picture the Order* (page 36) is a simple and useful flow chart for many purposes. It may be used like a storyboard with students sketching events in order or writing the steps.

For sequencing things that repeatedly cycle, the *Cycle Organizer* (page 37) is very useful. For a challenge, have students brainstorm a list of things that cycle repeatedly. Examples include the life cycle of a butterfly or seeds and plant growth.

A *Group Flow Chart Example* (page 38) will give students an idea about how to create a flow chart for their group's activities and assignments. The blank flow chart (page 39) that follows may be used for the group, but it will likely need to be modified according to the specifics of what the group and its individual members need to accomplish. Perhaps the first thing that a group should do is to create its own flow chart.

Causal Chains

Example

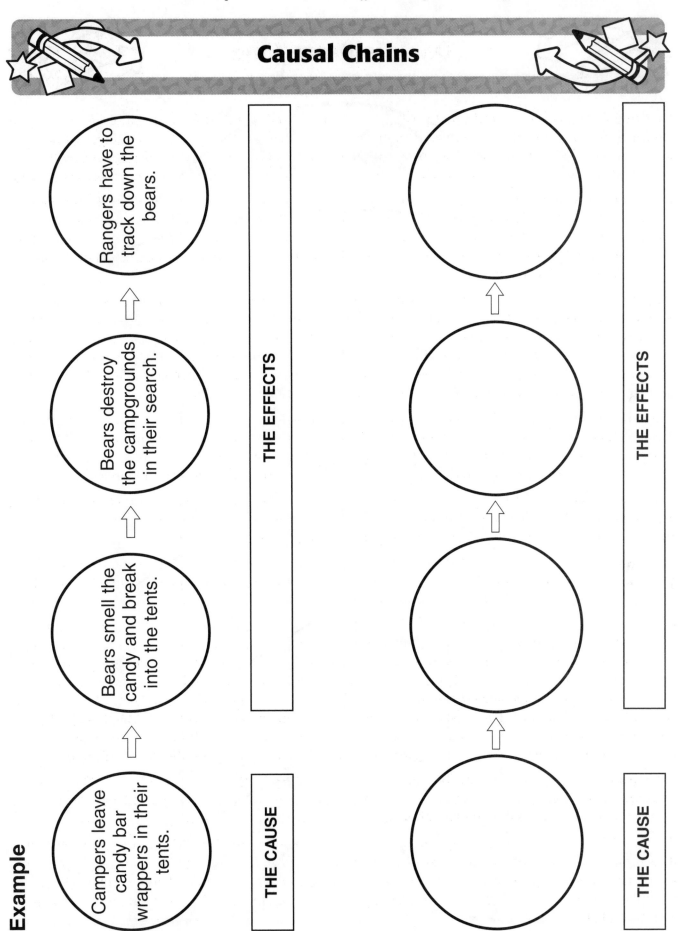

Rangers have to track down the bears.

Bears destroy the campgrounds in their search.

Bears smell the candy and break into the tents.

Campers leave candy bar wrappers in their tents.

THE EFFECTS

THE EFFECTS

THE CAUSE

THE CAUSE

Fishbone

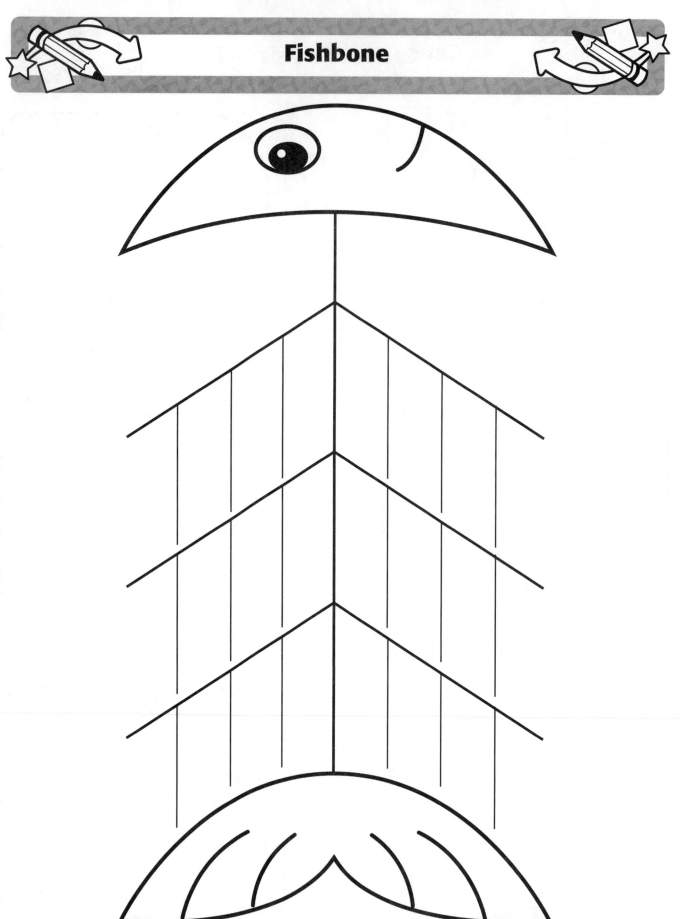

Cause and Effect Map

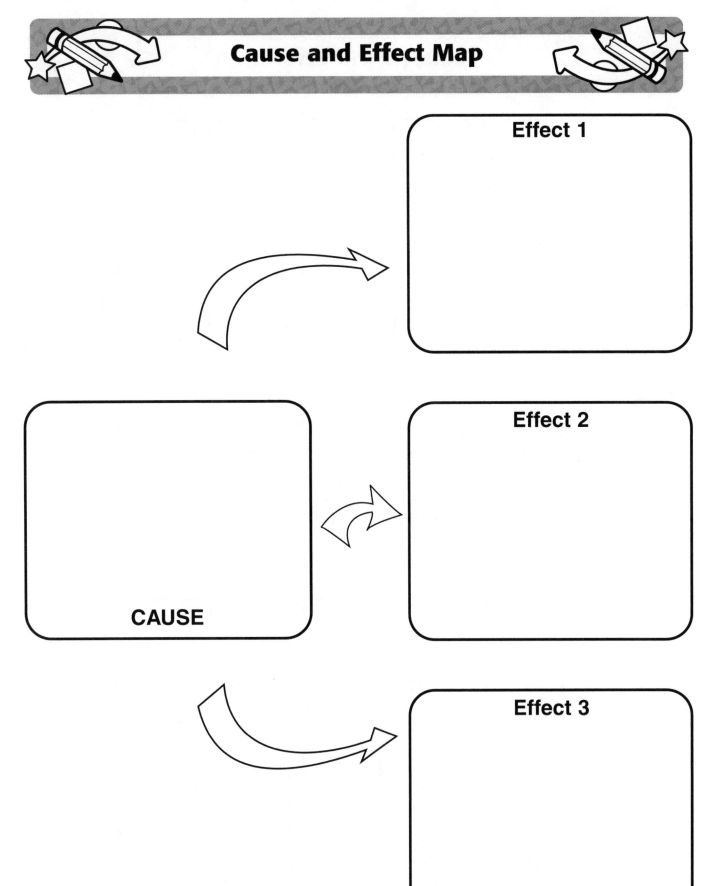

Effect 1

Effect 2

CAUSE

Effect 3

Causes and Effects

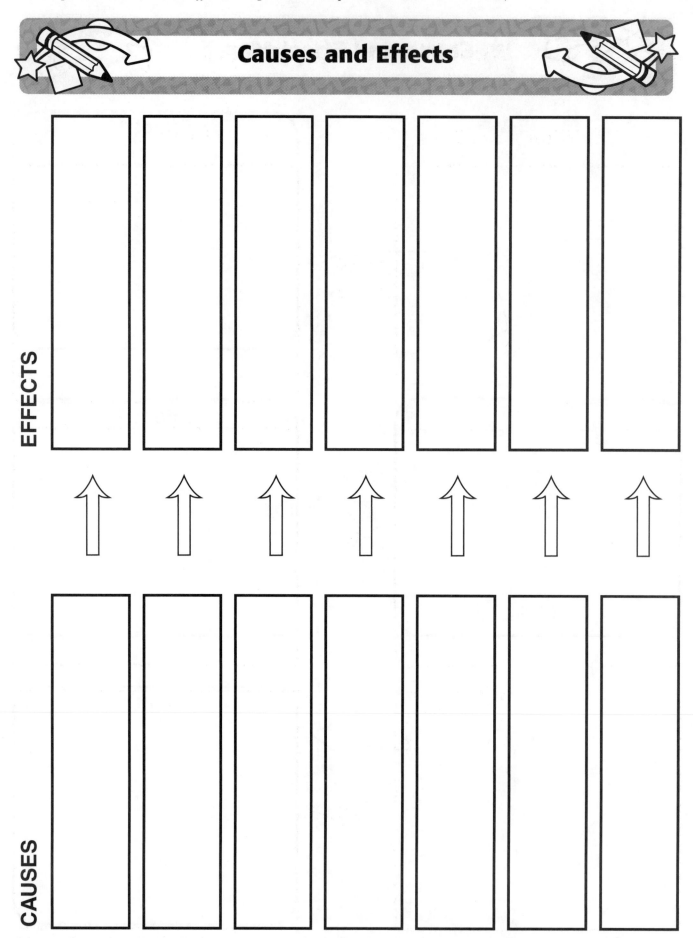

EFFECTS

CAUSES

What Would Happen If . . . ?

What If . . . ?   **Then . . .**

Herringbone

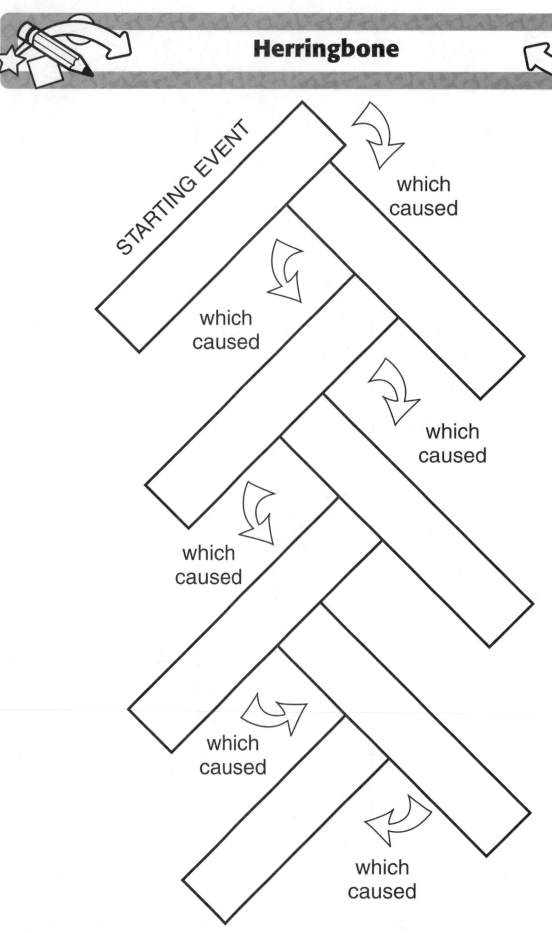

STARTING EVENT

which caused

which caused

which caused

which caused

which caused

which caused

Time Line

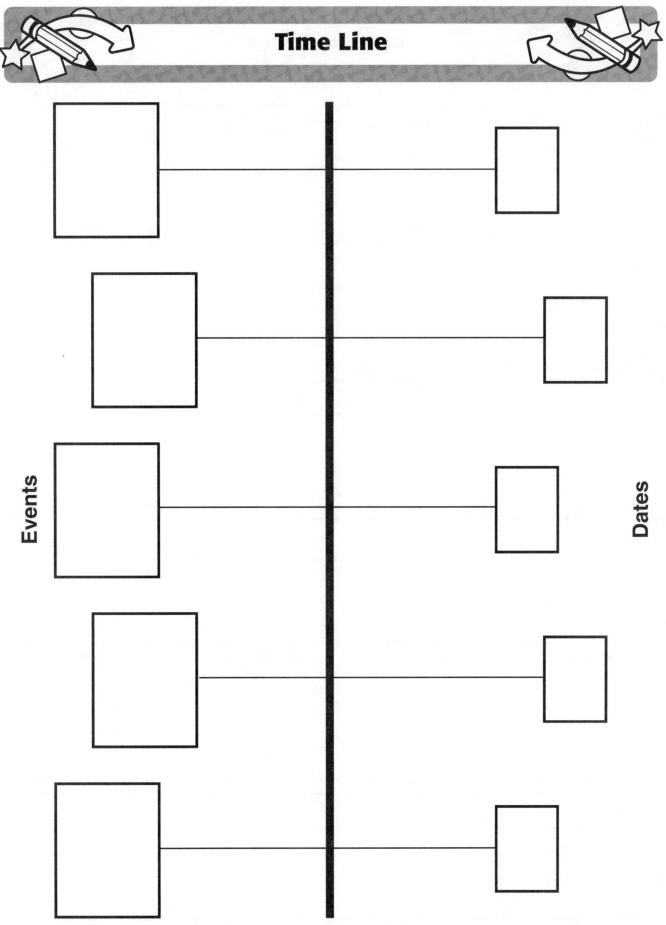

Events

Dates

 **Ideas in Order**

What I want to say/demonstrate/write about is . . .

First,

Second,

Third,

Fourth,

Finally,

Ideas Map

Purpose: _____

_____

1.

2.

4.

3.

5.

6.

Picture the Order

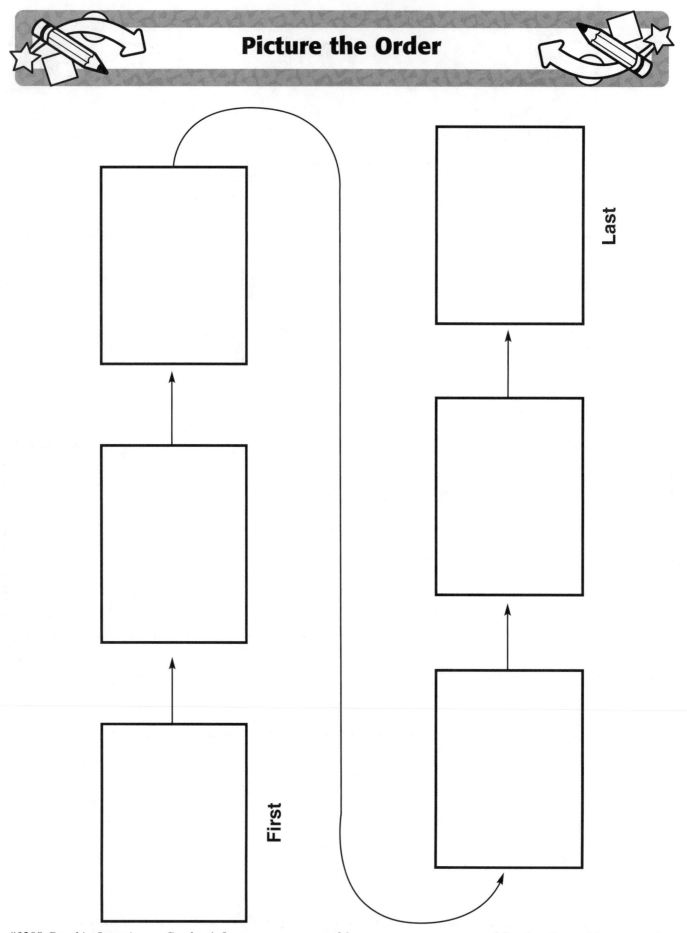

First

Last

Cycle Organizer

Type of Cycle: _____

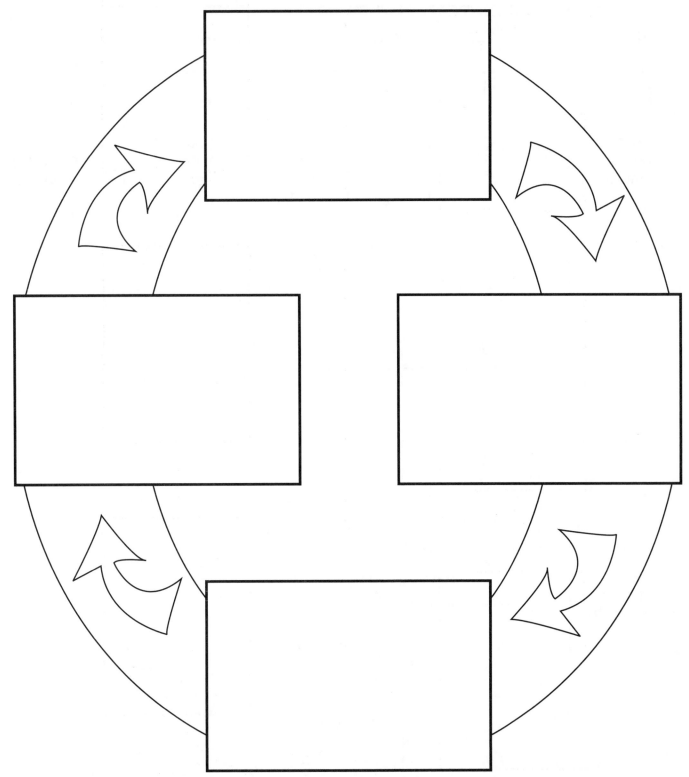

Group Flow Chart Example

PURPOSE/TOPIC: <u>Broadcast News Report on Local Bears</u>

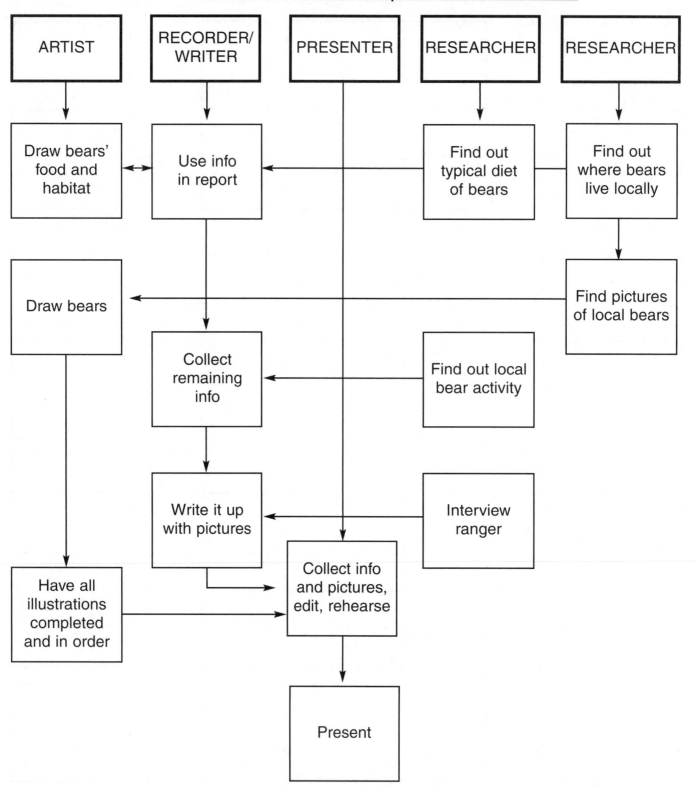

| ARTIST | RECORDER/WRITER | PRESENTER | RESEARCHER | RESEARCHER |

- Draw bears' food and habitat
- Use info in report
- Find out typical diet of bears
- Find out where bears live locally
- Draw bears
- Find pictures of local bears
- Collect remaining info
- Find out local bear activity
- Write it up with pictures
- Interview ranger
- Have all illustrations completed and in order
- Collect info and pictures, edit, rehearse
- Present

Group Flow Chart

Purpose/Topic: _____

As Compared to . . .

Graphic Organizers are essential for comparing and contrasting, analyzing details and choices, problem solving, and preparing to write. A simple chart, like the *Compare/Contrast Matrix* found on page 42 is a good place to start when needing to compare choices in order to make a decision, or when preparing to write an essay or research paper. The example, on page 41, will instruct students in how to use the matrix. Once students are familiar with the matrix, they can personalize the organizer to suit their needs, or create a new organizer.

Following the Compare and Contrast Matrix are two compare and contrast organizers, one for comparing and contrasting three things (*Difference/Similarities [Three Things]*, page 43) and one for comparing and contrasting four things (*Difference/Similarities [Four Things]*, page 44). These graphic organizers will be useful when doing more complex comparisons and contrasts. They will enable students to visualize and comprehend such complexities when used in a variety of subjects. As practice, and to allow students to familiarize themselves with such comparisons and contrasts, have them use the forms to compare themselves to friends, brothers and sisters, or classmates. Or compare simple topics, such as pets, sports, favorite books, etc.

Another way to compare and contrast two things would be with *The H-Chart* found on page 45. This chart is similar to a Venn diagram. Some students prefer this graphic organizer over others because of the sense of flow between the two sides. Venn diagrams have been around for quite some time and their usefulness inspires their longevity. One way to use them is in teaching students to write comparison and contrast essays. The ability to organize and write strong essays will serve them well throughout their school years. Use Venn diagrams for organizing thoughts during the prewriting stage. The *Prewriting Venn Example* on page 46 is filled in so that students can get an idea about how to do it. It is followed by a blank organizer on page 47 for students to use in order to write a strong comparison and contrast essay. This is also an opportunity to teach them the basics of a thesis essay. Introduce them to the concept and have them each write a thesis, as the main idea, before they fill in the Venn.

Graphic Organizers are very useful in making decisions and in problem solving. The *Decision Matrix Example* on page 48 will not only show students how to graph the pros and cons of a decision, it will show them the consequences of several choices. Teach students the meaning of pro and con so that they can use the terms in their evaluating processes as writers and thinkers. The Matrix example is followed, on page 49, with a blank one for them to use. They may also use this graphic organizer when writing to determine the choices of a character, or in social studies when considering what other choices there might be in any given situation. The *Decision Making Graph* (page 50) is similar but a bit more concise. We return to choosing pets with the final graphic organizer in this section. The *Thinking Matrix* (page 51) is a simple and versatile organizer which students can use in many ways for many different purposes.

Compare/Contrast Matrix Example

	Equipment	Clothing	Played On	
HOCKEY	puck stick goal	helmet skates padded jersey goalie's face mask	ice rink	
SOCCER	black and white ball goal	cleats shin guards jersey and shorts	grass field	

Compare/Contrast Matrix

Differences/Similarities (Three Things)

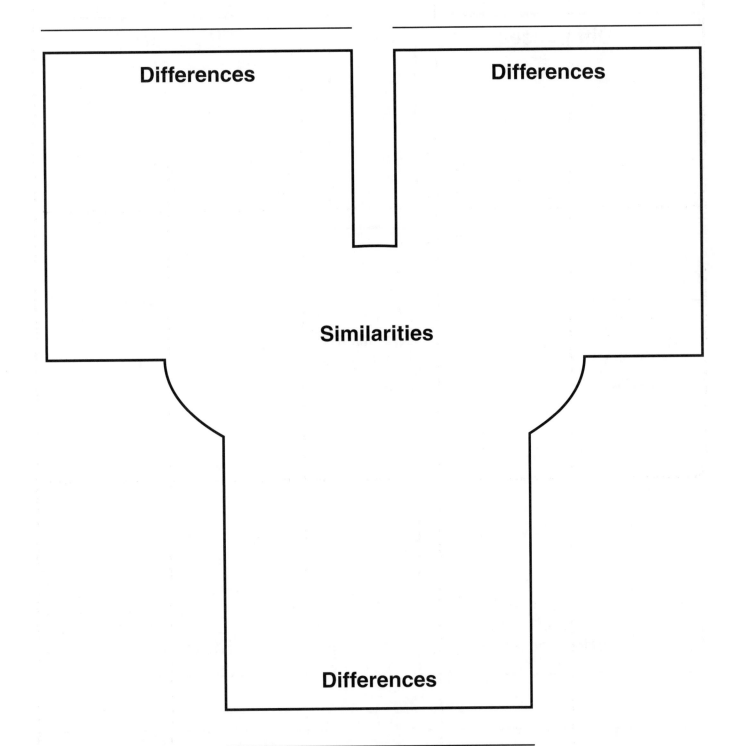

Differences

Differences

Similarities

Differences

Differences/Similarities (Four Things)

Differences

Differences

Similarities

Differences

Differences

The H-Chart

Directions: Label each side of the "H" with the two things you are comparing and contrasting. Under each label, list the ways each thing is different. In the center section of the "H," list the ways they are both the same.

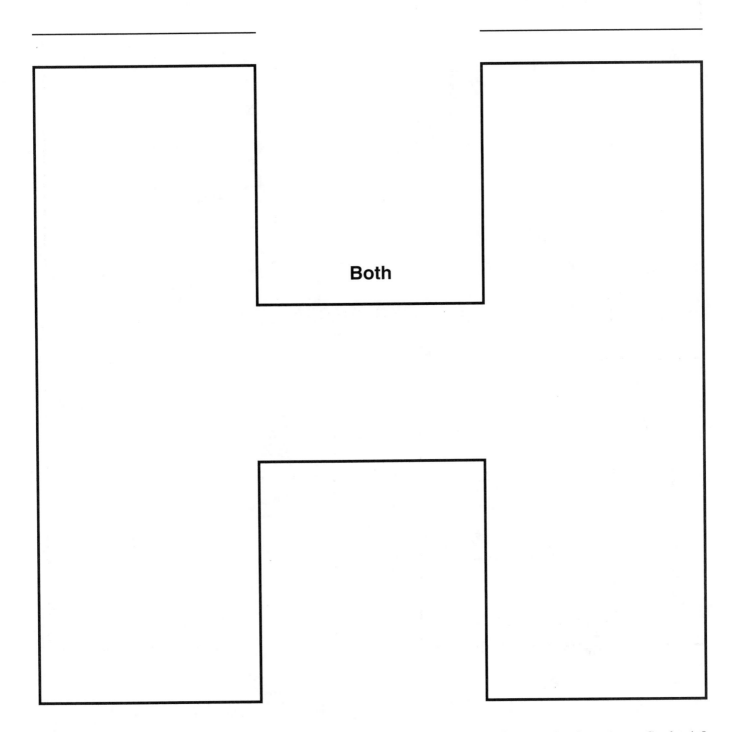

Both

Prewriting Venn Example

THESIS: Dogs and cats are very similar in many ways, but they are also very different.

DIFFERENCES

CATS

Bring you dead mice and birds

Groom themselves

Meow

Often want to be alone

Sleep on window sills, under cars

Usually don't get lost

Don't come when called

Don't walk on a leash

Like to climb

Get stuck in trees

Finicky eaters

Use litter box

BOTH

Fleas
Four-legged
Have tails
Wear collars
Make good pets
Affectionate
Playful
Need shots
Need food and water
Furry
Bite
Might get in fights with other animals
Hunt for prey
Need to visit the vet
Like to be scratched

DIFFERENCES

DOGS

Need to be bathed

Bark

Always want to be with people

Sleep on the floor or bed

Can sometimes get lost

Come when called

Walk on a leash

Can do tricks

Will eat anything

Need to clean up after them

CONCLUSION: While dogs and cats are a lot alike, a person should consider their differences before choosing a pet.

Prewriting Venn

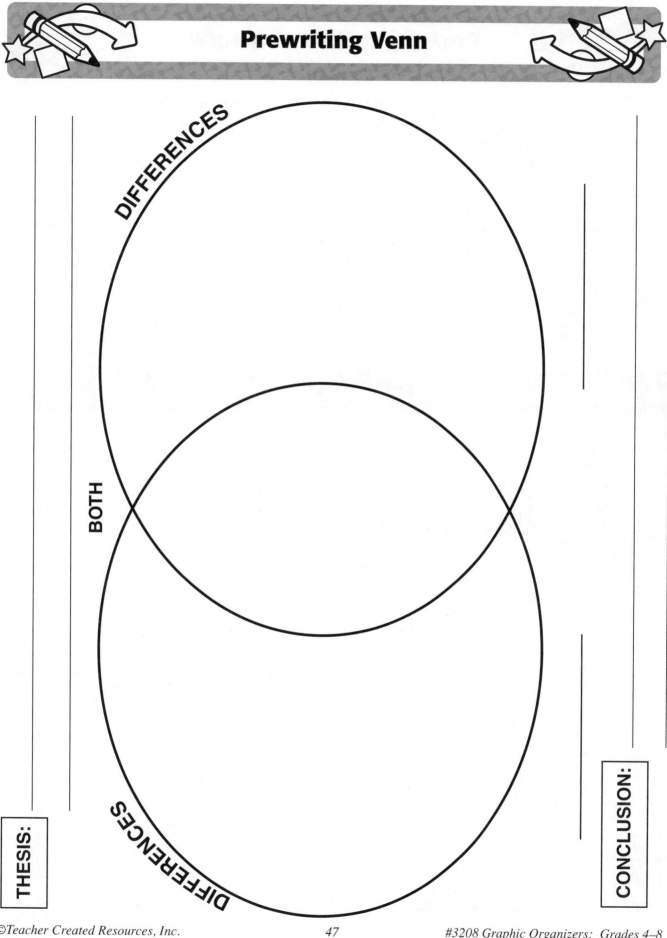

DIFFERENCES

BOTH

DIFFERENCES

THESIS:

CONCLUSION:

Decision Matrix Example

PROBLEM: Friends want you to help them cheat on a test

CHOICE
Help them

CHOICE
Just let them look over your shoulder

CHOICE
Not help them

+ PROS	– CONS
They will be your friends	You might get in trouble
They might like you for a while	Your parents would be disappointed in you
	You'd get a reputation as a cheater
	You might be failed
	You will feel bad

+ PROS	– CONS
You can pretend to be innocent	You might get caught
They might be your friends	Your friends might get mad at you
	You will feel bad
	You could get in a lot of trouble

+ PROS	– CONS
You'll stay out of trouble	Friends might not like you anymore
You'll know that you didn't cheat	
People will know you are honest	
Teachers will trust you	
You will feel good	
Your parents will be proud of you	

Decision Matrix

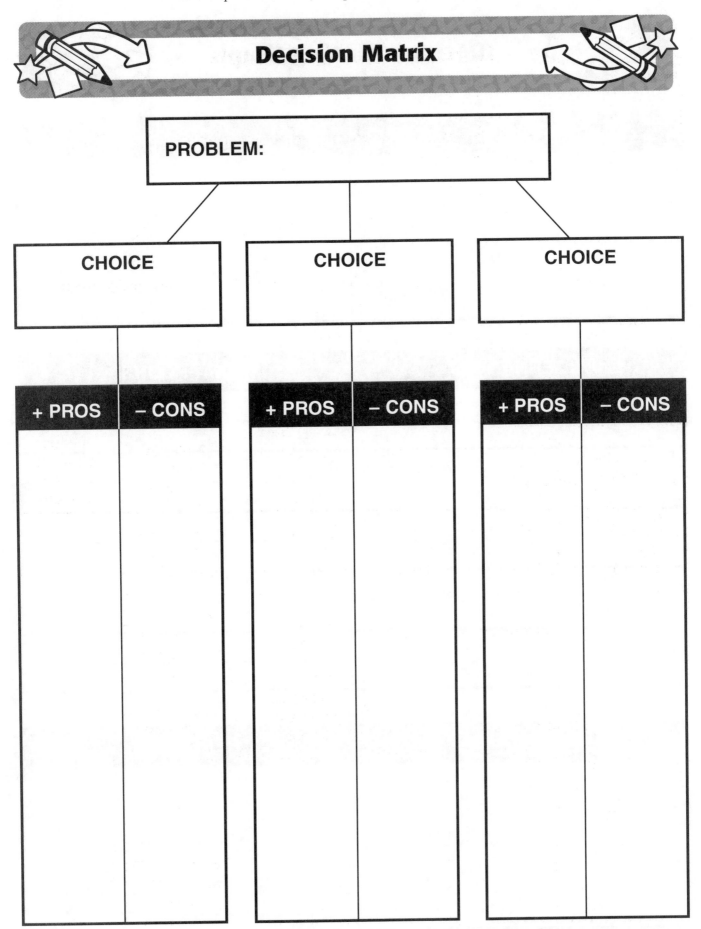

PROBLEM:

CHOICE

CHOICE

CHOICE

+ PROS	– CONS

+ PROS	– CONS

+ PROS	– CONS

Decision Making Graph

PROBLEM	GOALS

ALTERNATIVES	PROS + CONS –	
	+	
	–	
	+	
	–	
	+	
	–	
	+	
	–	
	+	
	–	

DECISION(S)	REASON(S)

 **Thinking Matrix**

Which Would Be the Best Pet for Me?

	good	bad	cost	work
CAT	cuddly +	allergic –	most of my allowance to feed –	clean litter box –
DOG	playful +	not allergic +	expensive food –	clean up after and walk – groom –
FISH	swims around +	can't play –	inexpensive +	clean fish bowl –
HAMSTER	cuddly + and playful +	not happy to see me –	affordable +	clean cage— food and water daily –

Who Gets the Biggest Piece?

Students will be able to sink their teeth into this section as various forms of graphs make it easy for them to visualize and organize information. Pie graphs enable students to readily access quantitative information. Students come pre-equipped with an interest in who gets the largest piece of the pie. A pizza pie, made from colorful construction paper and appropriately labeled, can help students to comprehend fractions, percentages, and other math concepts including amounts of time, portions of a whole, or preferences. If possible, a demonstration with a real piece of pie, or a bar graph cut into a flat pan of baked goodies will make the learning even more memorable. This section begins with a pie graph dividing up the students' favorite subjects. Have the students discuss and list the subjects, first, and then have them each vote once for their favorites. Tally the results, as a class, figure the percentages, and create a pie graph on the board, then have students create individual ones. Using the same *Pie Graph Organizer* (page 53), challenge students to divide up how they spend their daytime hours, or choose a bar graph with information, and covert the information to a pie graph.

A *Bar Graph Organizer Example* is found on page 54. The title of this one is "Our Favorite Kinds of Books" and it is an example for students. A blank organizer follows on page 55, but because bar graphs vary so much, depending on the information they contain, encourage your students to create bar graphs whenever possible. Bar graphs can be horizontal, or vertical, or even diagonal or plaid! Students can be very creative when making bar graphs, and make the bars different objects, such as a line of cars if graphing traffic patterns, or long baby bottles if graphing babysitting hours. An example of a line graph can be found on page 56. Students can refer to it when creating their own line graphs. For a challenge, have students graph the same information in three ways: a pie graph, a bar graph and a line graph. Point out to students how a line graph can organize more complex information. For instance, the babysitting hours of several students portrayed on one line graph. Help them, to see how a line graph facilitates comparison.

Pyramids are a popular graphic organizer. These days there are several food pyramids to consult. Bring some in for students to examine. Have them keep food journals, and then use the blank *Pyramid* on page 57 to create their own, actual, food pyramid. Students can also use the pyramid to organize writing, by putting the main idea or thesis in the top portion and supporting details below. They may divide up a pyramid to use for biographical or autobiographical information. A pyramid organizer can also be used for a book report. Put the title and author name at the top and the bottom would be the place to write a synopsis. Divide a pyramid into five sections, label each section for one of the five senses, and have students fill them in to describe a setting or season as a prewriting activity.

Senses can also be graphed on a grid such as the *Sensory Imaging* found on page 58. Have them use the information in their writing when describing settings, atmosphere, characters, whether fictional or historical.

The *Concept Wheel*, page 59, is used to graph the 5 Ws and 1 H to prepare to write or give an oral presentation. Concept wheels can be used in many other ways, as well. Simply use the inner circle for labels, and fill in the larger sections with the ideas or thoughts.

The *Why? Pie* (pages 60 and 61) encourages students to listen and pay attention, and encourages their natural curiosities. You may wish to introduce the Why? Pie concept with a brainstorming session and a demonstration. The best learning takes place when students are curious and motivated to find the answers to their questions.

Pie Graph Organizer

Example

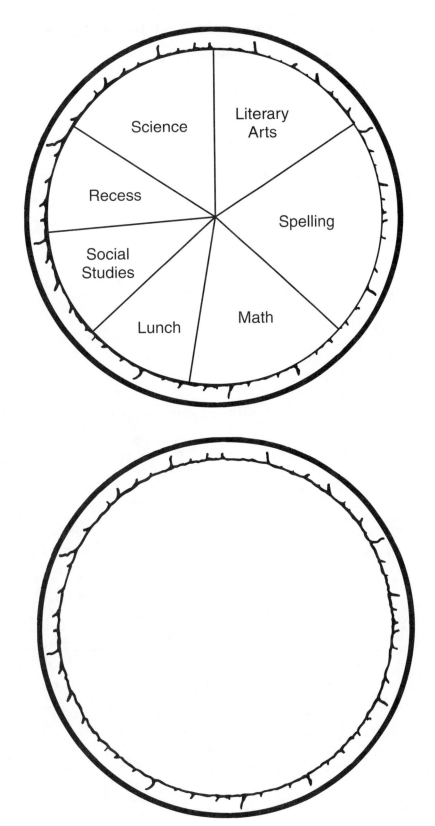

Bar Graph Organizer Example

TITLE: Our Favorite Kinds of Books

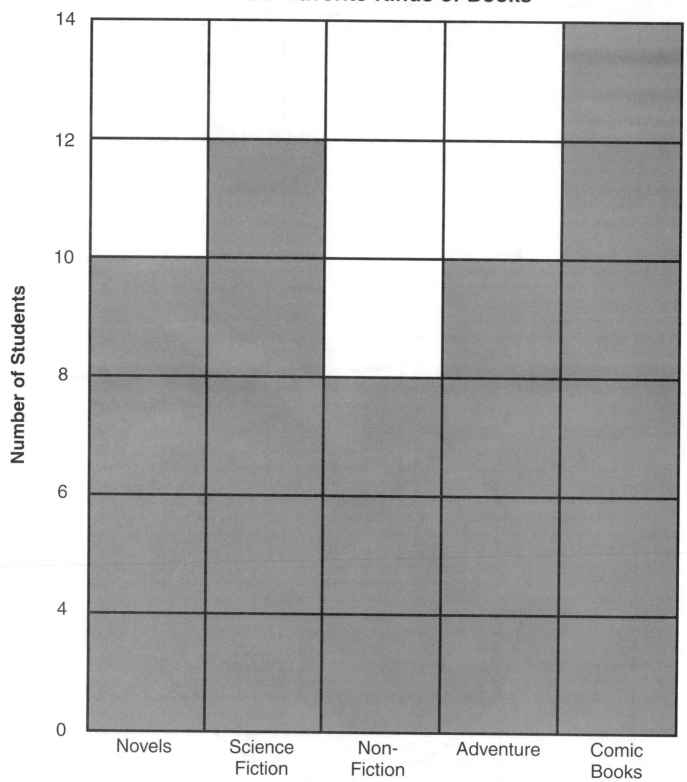

Bar Graph Organizer

TITLE: _____

Line Graph Organizer

What do you want to show in your graph? _____

_____

How will you show this information?_____

_____

After you place dots at the correct spots on your graph, connect them with lines.

EXAMPLE OF A LINE GRAPH TO SHOW HOW MUCH HOMEWORK STUDENTS TURN IN
(Amount of homework is shown in percentages over a period of ten months.)

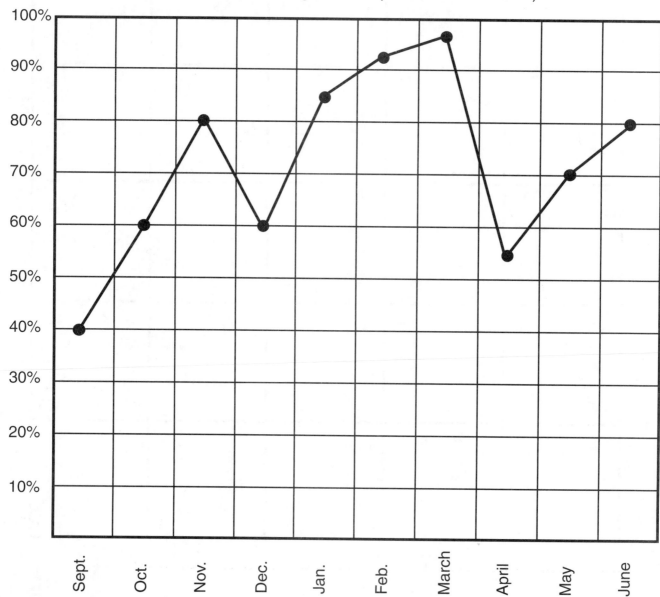

Pyramid

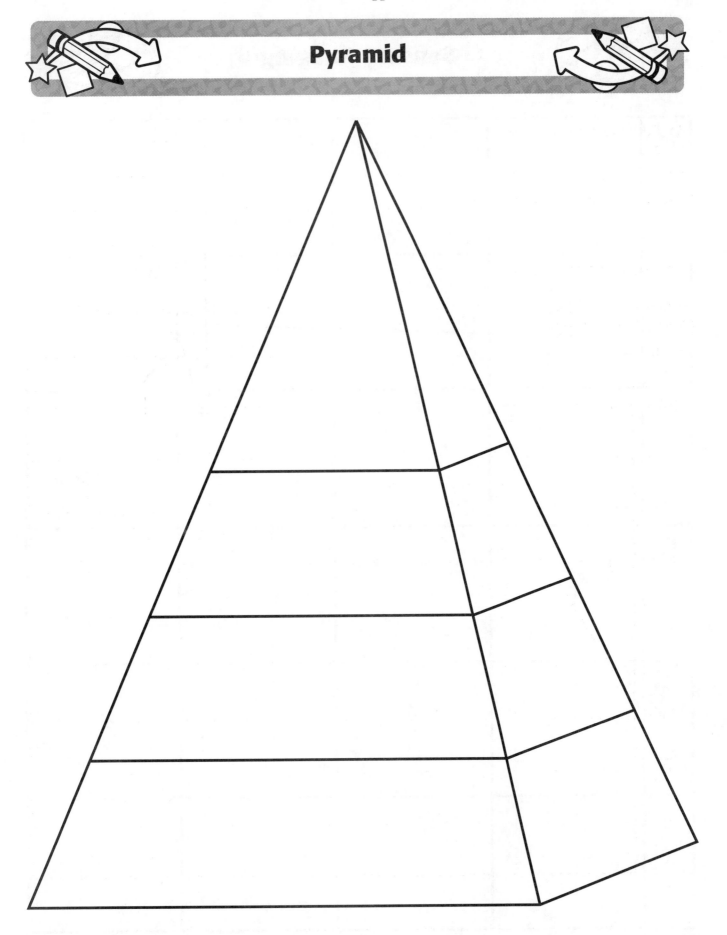

Who Gets the Biggest Piece? (Pies, Pyramids, Graphs, and Grids)

Sensory Imaging

Tastes				
Sounds				
Smells				
Feels				
Looks				
Item				

Concept Wheel

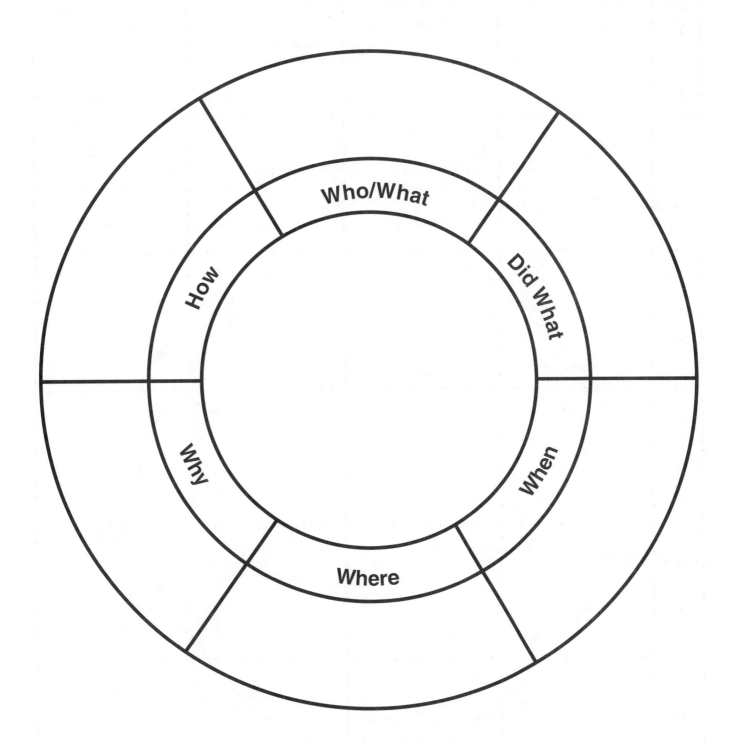

Why? Pie

You can use the Why? Pie strategy to help students identify essential relationships between objects or concepts. Model the strategy by having students read an expository passage and then ask questions that begin with the word "Why" and can only be answered by inference (the answer is not directly stated in the article). Then have students read further and work in pairs to come up with why questions about the material and to discuss possible responses to their questions. After that, they can exchange questions with another pair and develop responses to those questions as well. Here's an example of a student's Why? Pie after reading this article:

> Floods happen when too much water runs into a stream or river. The stream or river gets so high it goes right over its banks. Floods drown people and animals. Floods can wash away houses, cars, and bridges. They hurt crops and carry away topsoil. For thousands of years people have tried to stop floods.

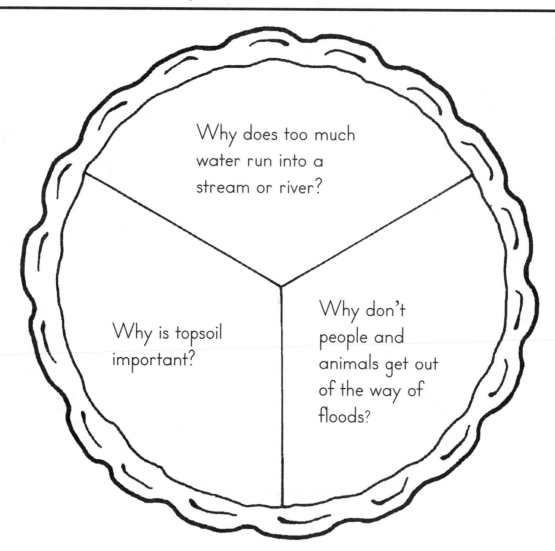

Why? Pie

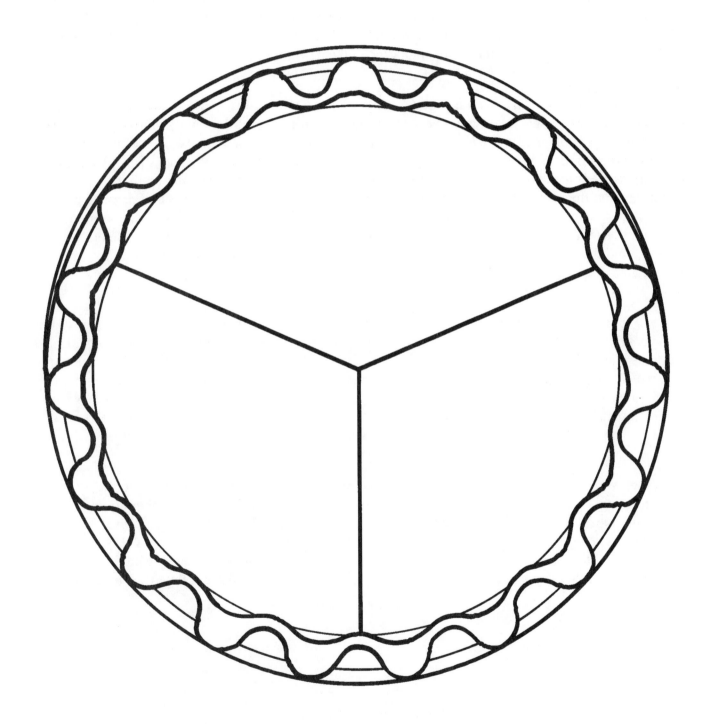

In My Opinion . . .

It is very important for students to comprehend, as soon as they are able to, the concept of a thesis or main idea, and supporting points. It is a template, as it were, that they will use throughout their school careers. Their ability to visualize this concept early on will enable them to be strong students when it is time to express their ideas in a variety of forums, especially the thesis essay. The *Target* on page 64 will help students visualize the importance of the main idea bull's eye. Have students write their main ideas in the center circle with the details radiating outward within the concentric circles.

The graphic organizer, *Blueprint*, on page 65 makes the structure of the edifice that students will "build" (paragraph, essay, report, etc.) very clear to them. If they each follow the blueprint, the final product will be as planned. The *Fishbone (5 Ws and 1 H)* organizer on page 66, is useful in organizing writing or reporting, as it reminds students to include each aspect of the 5 Ws and 1 H. It is also useful in other ways. If the text is removed before photocopying, students can write the main idea along the center line and the supporting details along the sides. The *Stair Step* organizer found on page 68 is one of the more unusual organizers, and it can be useful in several different ways. Its most common, fluid, and sequential way is demonstrated on page 67. Other ways would include putting the main idea on the top step, and the supporting details of two subtopics down each side. A conclusion could then be written across the bottom, or inside the stairs.

Jellyfish (page 69) is a popular organizer. The organic quality of created writing can be demonstrated in the actual structure of a jellyfish, so pictures might reinforce the concept. The *Jellyfish* organizer is useful as a template for a typical five-paragraph essay. Students can write the main point in the top box, which would be the introductory or thesis paragraph. The supporting paragraphs are represented by the three boxes, and the supporting details dangle from the three boxes. For younger students writing a paragraph, the top box would contain the introductory or topic sentence. The three boxes would be for three supporting points, each to take a sentence. The details for each point are below.

Main Idea Webs (pages 70–72) have been, well, the main idea all along. Whether clustering, brainstorming, or outlining, the main idea is the central focus. The tricky part is lining up the supporting ideas so that it all makes sense and flows in a logical manner. *Main Idea Web* on page 70 represents a prewriting activity for a report. This is followed by two blank webs, *I Need Support!* (page 71) and *Web Plus Subs* (page 72). Any kind of web can be created, however, easily and quickly. Use these blanks for practice and encourage students to create their own webs any time they need to plot a plan.

In My Opinion . . .

Sometimes, the best way to convince students that they can write a strong, persuasive essay or paragraph, is to remind them that they already have arguing skills. Ask them about the last time they tried to convince their parents that they deserved an increase in allowance, or that they should be allowed to stay up later for some particular reason. If their persuasive arguments were to be listed on the board, they might be surprised to see that they know how to support their points already. Instruct them that a persuasive essay is one in which they take a stance ("I need more allowance."), choose their strongest supports (". . . because the costs of things have gone up, because I am older and have more responsibilities, and because I am buying more of my own school things and clothes."). For practice, give them topics about which they will have strong opinions. The graphic organizer on page 73, *Strong Support Writing*, will provide them with the structure.

We moaned when our teachers insisted that we outline our essays and reports first, but, they have proven over and over again to be a good way to organize our thoughts, stay on topic, and create a finished product that requires little revision. They will prove themselves once more with today's students. A simple outline for a three-point thesis (essay for older students, paragraph for younger) is found on page 74. Expand the concept with more complex essays, adding 1., 2., and 3., etc., and lowercase letters as topics and subtopics are broken down into more and more details. Have beginning outliners pick topics that are familiar to them such as their pets, their favorite sports, etc. As they progress they can use outlines for more formal essays and research reports.

Students will be repeatedly exposed to the five-paragraph essay in high school and college. The graphic organizer, *Five-Paragraph Essay* (page 75) will help them to more fully visualize the structure, thereby assisting a smooth transition between idea and expression of idea. *Persuasion Plan*, on page 76, is another graphic way to see how to arrange an argument. Have students use the organizer to prepare an opinion or argument presentation. Using editorials or letters to the editor from the opinion section of a newspaper, have students use an organizer to analyze what they read. Did the writers follow an organized format of any kind in their arguments? If some did and if some did not seem to, which writers had the more convincing letters or editorials?

Target

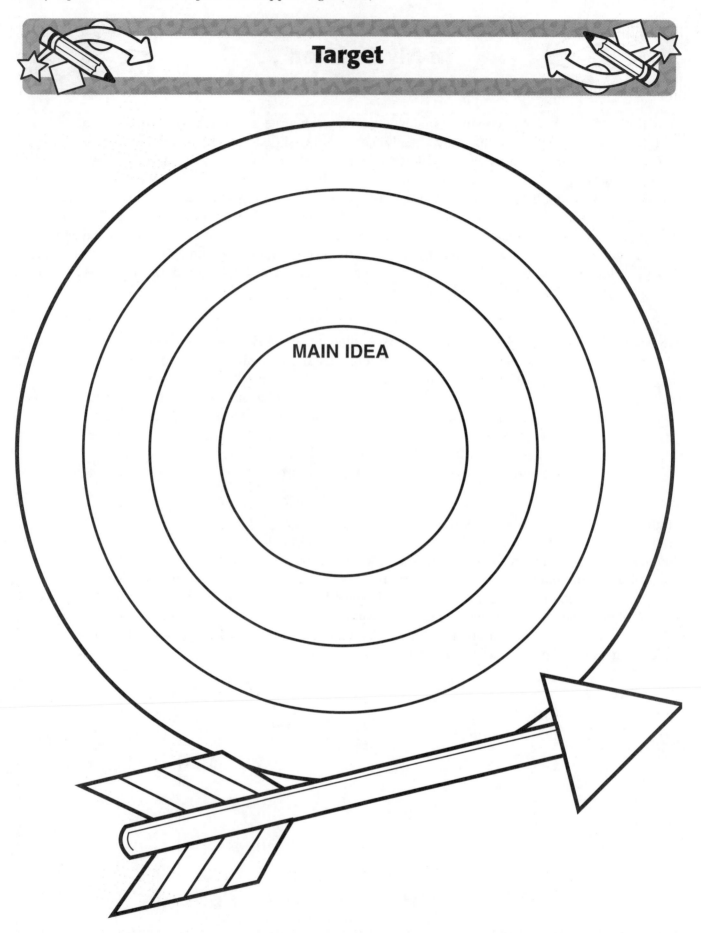

MAIN IDEA

Blueprint

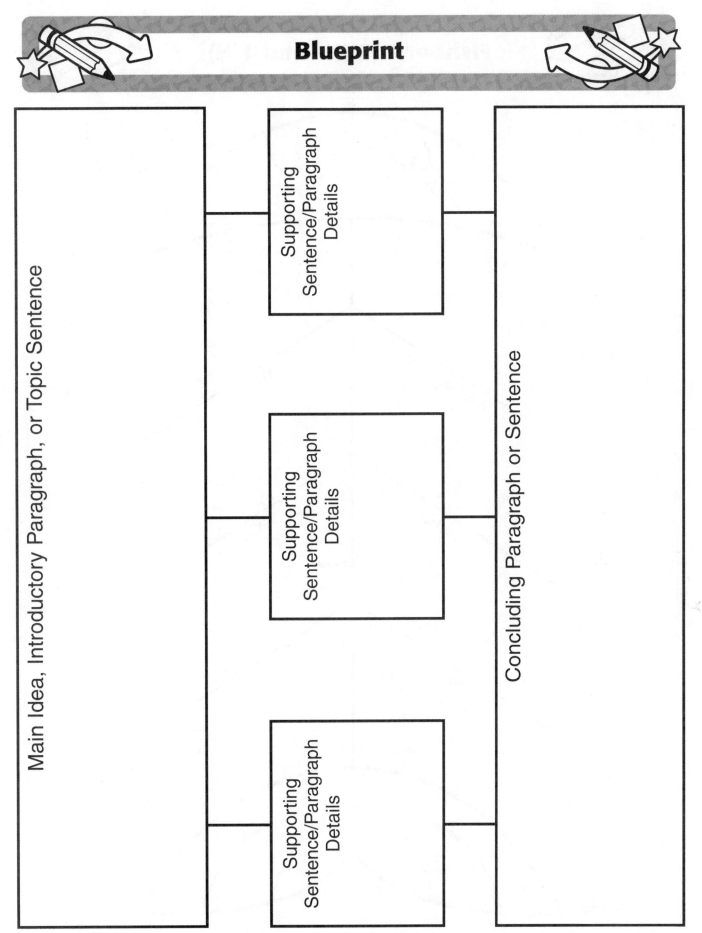

Main Idea, Introductory Paragraph, or Topic Sentence

Supporting Sentence/Paragraph Details

Supporting Sentence/Paragraph Details

Supporting Sentence/Paragraph Details

Concluding Paragraph or Sentence

Fishbone (5 Ws and 1 H)

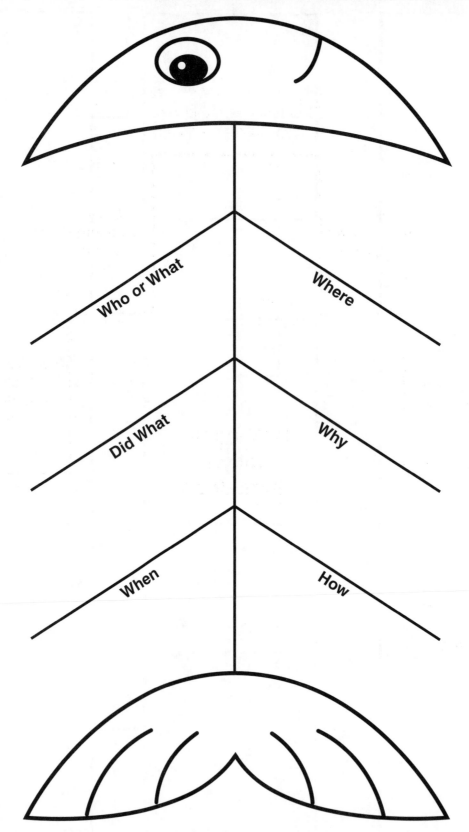

Who or What

Where

Did What

Why

When

How

Stair Step Example

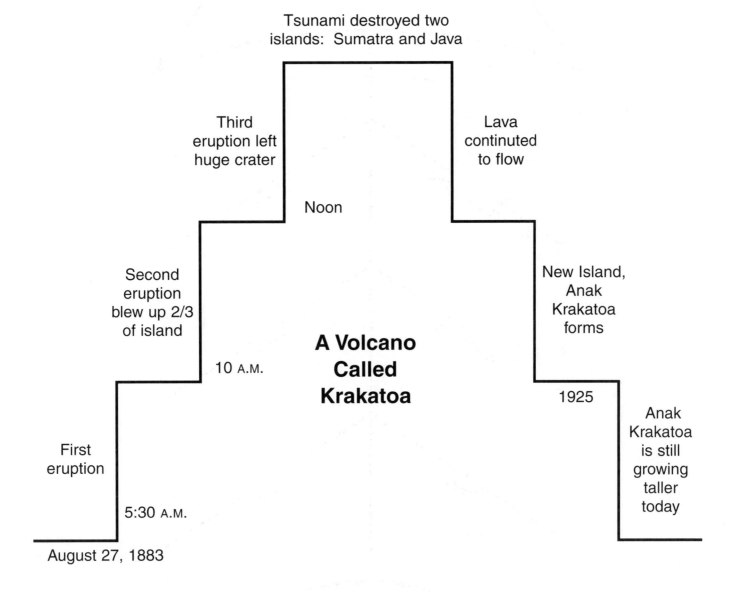

Tsunami destroyed two
islands: Sumatra and Java

Third
eruption left
huge crater

Lava
continued
to flow

Noon

Second
eruption
blew up 2/3
of island

New Island,
Anak
Krakatoa
forms

**A Volcano
Called
Krakatoa**

10 A.M.

1925

First
eruption

Anak
Krakatoa
is still
growing
taller
today

5:30 A.M.

August 27, 1883

 **Stair Step**

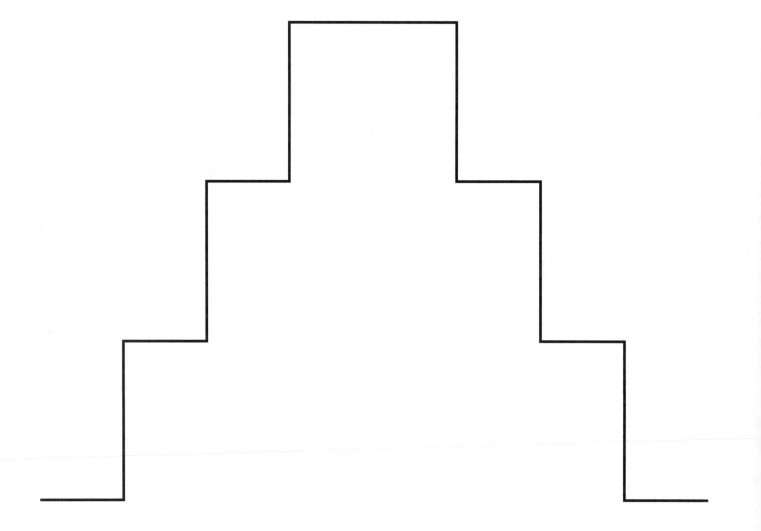

Jellyfish

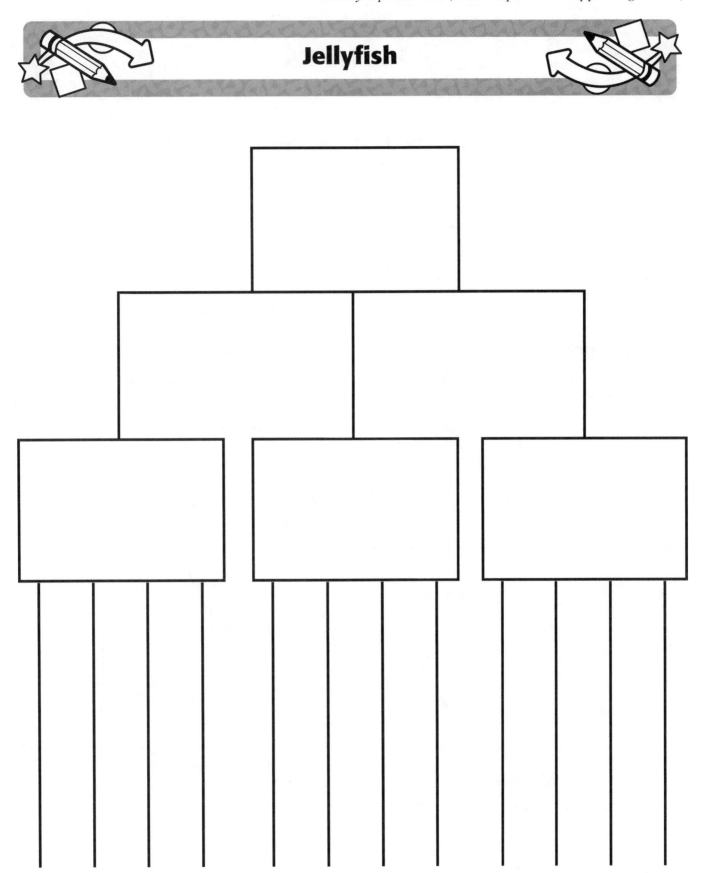

Main Idea Web

The Five Senses

The back of the brain is where seeing is located.

Supporting Detail

Different parts of your brain allow your senses to work.

Supporting Detail

We use our ability to taste, see, hear, feel, and smell to learn about the world.

Main Idea

The part of the brain that controls hearing is located over your ears.

Supporting Detail

Hearing and seeing are human's most important senses.

Supporting Detail

I Need Support!

Support

Support

Proposition

Support

Support

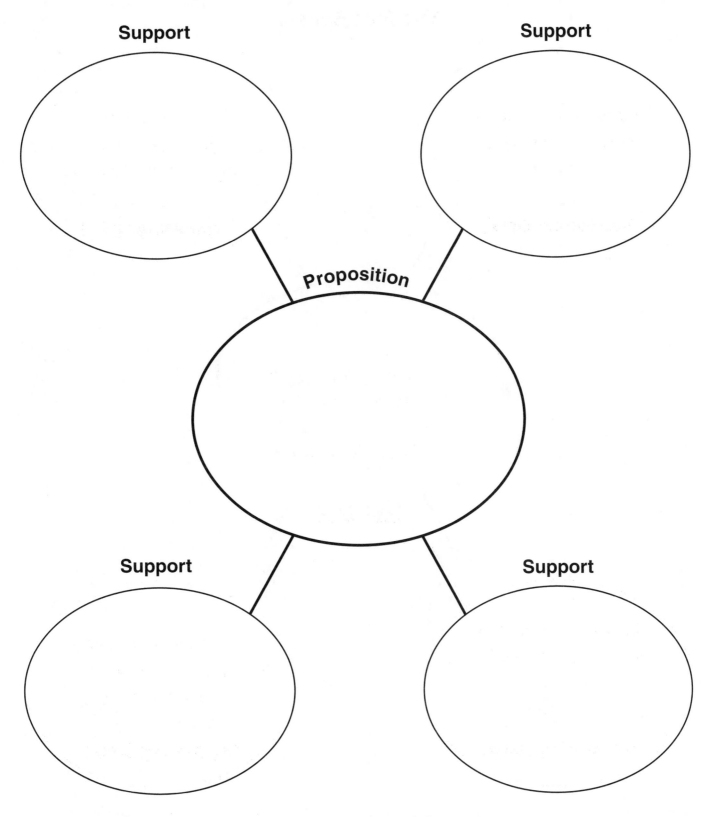

Web Plus Subs

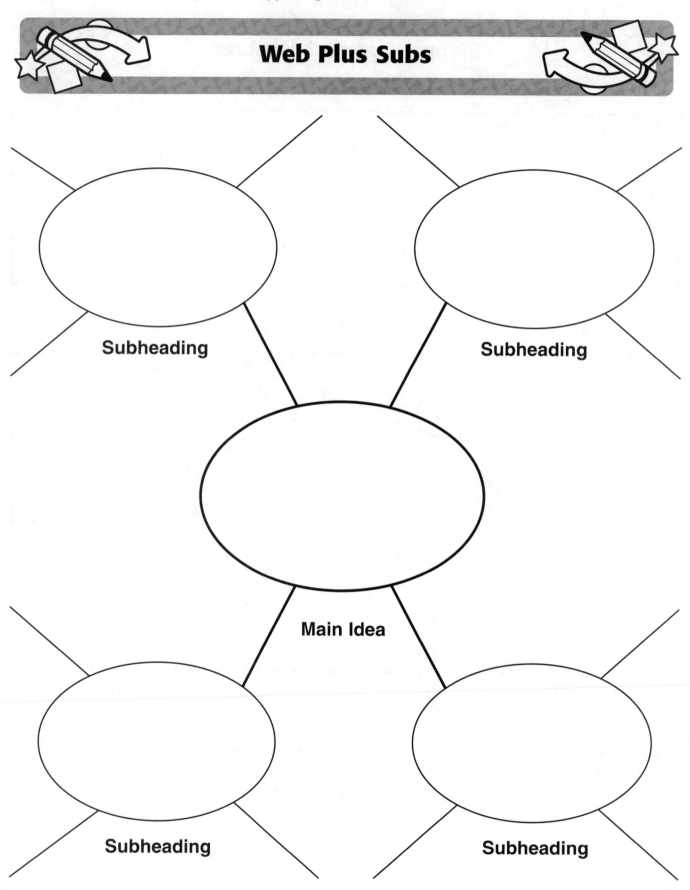

Subheading

Subheading

Main Idea

Subheading

Subheading

Strong Support Writing

I will prove that . . .

First of all, . . .

-
-
-

Secondly, . . .

-
-
-

And finally, . . .

-
-
-

Therefore, . . .

Outlining

Title: _____

I. Introductory Paragraph

A.

B.

C.

II. Supporting Body Paragraph

A.

B.

C.

III. Supporting Body Paragraph

A.

B.

C.

IV. Supporting Body Paragraph

A.

B.

C.

V. Concluding Paragraph

A.

B.

C.

Five-Paragraph Essay

Main Idea, Introductory and Thesis Paragraph

Support/Proof Details

Support/Proof Details

Support/Proof Details

Summary/Conclusion

Persuasion Plan

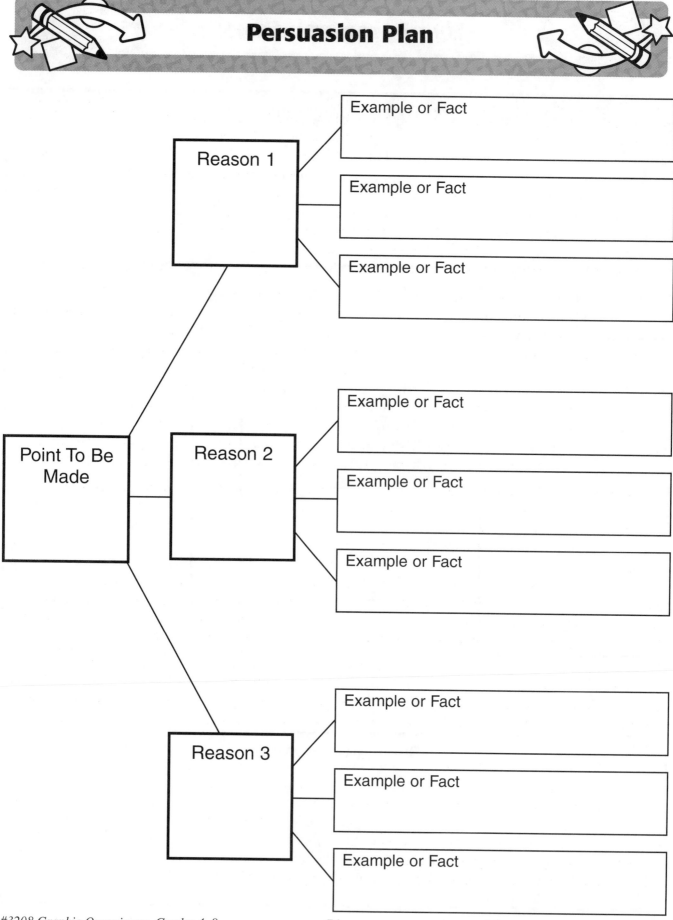

Where Are We Now?

Maps are useful, necessary, and most welcome for determining where one has traveled, where one is located, and where one wishes to go. This section contains graphic organizers that facilitate comprehension of concepts and the organization of concepts in the format of mind maps and variations of hierarchy and schema of information. One important aspect of such learning "travel" is that of understanding what one wishes to learn, and predicting what one will learn. As travel brochures assist the traveler anticipating new vistas, so do these graphic organizers. The section begins with a simple and straightforward organizer, *Chapter Titles,* page 78. This is a useful organizer for younger students picking up an interesting nonfiction book at the library. Extend the number of chapters to create an organizer for older students beginning a new, complex textbook. Keep their predictions on file to look at when they have finished their books. They may wish to record an update of their learning from their expanded views.

A *K-W-L Chart* (page 79) is a classic essential for charting new territory. Have plenty of copies on hand for use in many different situations. Remember to bring them out when introducing a new unit of study, and also, as an activity tied into research. *What I Learned* (page 80) continues in the same direction with a graphic organizer that facilitates comprehension and analysis. Have younger students fill in the organizer after reading a short article, such as those found in children's news magazines or other kinds of children's magazines. Have them fill in the first portion (about what they already knew) before reading to make the experience more meaningful. Have an interesting class discussion about what surprises the students found in their reading. The form can also be used for oral presentations, short videos, etc. More complex articles will challenge older and more capable students. The form could also be used for books and for pre- and post-research report writing.

The important K-W-L train of thought continues with the *K-W-L Variation* on page 81. This is a graphic organizer that is very suitable to younger students reading nonfiction books in their areas of interest. It even gives them an opportunity to express their learning in drawing. Older students will also enjoy the form because of its straightforward approach and, especially, for the opportunity to think of unanswered questions. Focus a discussion on what questions they felt were unanswered, and how to go about finding the answers. The drawing portion of the organizer can be modified or eliminated for more capable students. One thing to keep in mind when modifying the drawing portion is that often nonfiction books can use a drawing or diagram or two. A capable student may appreciate the challenge of drawing a battle map, a diagram of a robot or rocket, or a surfboard with its parts labeled.

The *Story Map,* page 82, enables students to analyze a story. This is useful for reading comprehension and for expressing what has been read, such as in the form of a book report. The map is also useful for writers and has been used in writing classes. If students use the form to create a route for a story, they will have a stronger, more compelling story. Good stories have a conflict and a character who must overcome.

The *Knowledge Tier* (pages 83 and 84) will be a vehicle for students in that it will take them to more complex ways of thinking. They will discover that in any field there are layers of knowledge. They will never exhaust the amount of knowledge in an area of interest, and so therefore, learning is an adventure. Have them practice filling out the organizer for many different topics. Allow individual students to become experts in areas of interest. Have them fill out the organizer with layers of terminology which they will review with the class in oral presentations. Students may enjoy being experts of their favorite topics. These experts can make themselves available to younger classes as called upon.

Chapter Titles

Directions: List the chapter titles in your book. Name something you will learn in each chapter. What do you think is the main idea of this book?

1. Chapter title: _____

    I will learn _____

2. Chapter title: _____

    I will learn _____

3. Chapter title: _____

    I will learn _____

4. Chapter title: _____

    I will learn _____

5. Chapter title: _____

    I will learn _____

The main idea is _____

_____

K-W-L Chart

I Know	I Wonder	I Learned

What I Learned

Before I started reading about _____, I knew

_____

_____

_____

In the article, I learned _____

_____

_____

_____

_____

I also learned _____

_____

_____

_____

I was surprised _____

_____

_____

_____

K-W-L Variation

Directions: Write the title and topic of the book. Then follow the directions in each box.

Title: _____

Topic: _____

What do you know before reading this book?

1. _____
   _____
2. _____
   _____

What did you learn from reading this book?

1. _____
   _____
2. _____
   _____

Draw a picture and label one thing you learned from your reading on the back of this paper.

Write two questions you have about the topic that weren't answered in this book.

1. _____
   _____
2. _____
   _____

Story Map

Title:

Author:

Characters:

Setting:

Somebody (main character):

Wants (what main character is trying to do):

But (the conflict/problem that stands in the way):

So (how the main character solves the problem):

Knowledge Tier Example

cytoplasm

mitochondria

vacuoles

EXPERT KNOWLEDGE

cell membrane

cell nucleus

invertebrate

vertebrate

exoskeleton

USEFUL KNOWLEDGE

common features of all animals

organisms

cell

energy

waste

life cycle

reproduce

environment

growth

ESSENTIAL KNOWLEDGE

Class-generated Questions

- What are the common features of all animals?

- What are organisms?

- How does energy relate to animals?

- What is waste?

- What is a life cycle?

- What does it mean to reproduce?

- What is environment and what does it have to do with animals?

- What are a cell membrane and a cell nucleus?

- What is the difference between an invertebrate and a vertebrate?

- What is an exoskeleton?

Knowledge Tier

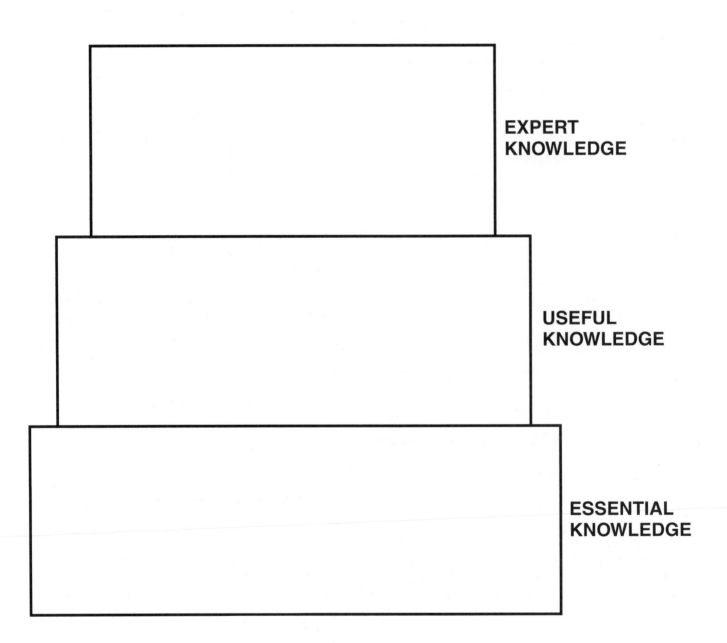

EXPERT KNOWLEDGE

USEFUL KNOWLEDGE

ESSENTIAL KNOWLEDGE

Creative Tools

A student's favorite subject is, of course, him or herself! *My Own Coat of Arms* (page 86) gives students an opportunity to create a work of art about their own lives. These organizers would make a great display around the room, especially at the beginning of the school year. The same organizer may be extended when applied to historical or fictional subjects.

The *Acrostic Grid*, found on page 87, will be useful for many subjects. To use, choose a topic, or have students choose a topic, and write it down the left-hand column. For instance, t-r-e-e-s. All lines need not be used, and the grid can be expanded for more capable students. For each line, students will add words, phrases, sentences, or even the lines of a poem to utilize that letter of the alphabet. For instance, T = tall, R = red, E = elegant, E = evergreen, S = shade.

Continuing with the alphabet, page 88 features an *Alphabet Organizer*. To use, assign a topic and students are to fill in as many words as they can think of to fit each square. For instance, if the topic is Literature, then the **A** box might contain the words: *alliteration*, *allegory*, and *assonance*. The **P** box could be for: *parody*, *plot*, *point of view*, *prose*, etc. Use the form to play games similar to Scattergories, as well.

Imagine What's Missing (page 89) is a fun exercise in sequence as well as a means of introducing students to the storyboard concept. Students may fill in the blank spaces with drawings to complete the sequences, or they may write what would happen in each blank. Have students create their own storyboard sequences with blank spaces and trade with a partner to fill them in.

The *Storyboard* organizer follows on page 90. Instruct students in the uses of storyboards. Let them know that they are used in many ways in the world. Of course, cartoonists and animators use them, but they are useful to others, as well. Writers sometimes use them to graphically organize a scene, or an entire novel. Managers or committee chairs use them to organize a sequence of events. Photographers use them to create a plan for a photo shoot so that they will be sure to get every shot. They are useful in story writing, analyzing stories, and planning the steps in a presentation. Have students use them to prepare a graphic outline, as it were, for a story, either fictional, or a personal experience. For more practice, have them use storyboards to prepare a skit.

Comic Strip (page 91) features a blank comic strip. It may be used for vocabulary word use, to illustrate an event in a student's life, or an event in history. It may also be used for sequencing: steps in a how-to or the order of the school day, etc., with characters describing what is happening. For fun, let students try creating a funny cartoon strip. They will find it challenging, and they will also learn to organize by sticking to the graph.

Your students won't realize that they are increasing, vocabulary, writing, and organizational skills when they each have a position on the classroom newspaper. Use *The Newsroom* organizers such as those found on pages 92 and 93 to assist in their reporting and publishing. Have them report on the classroom activities, birthdays, events, and learning. Rotate the positions so that each student has a full range of experience in journalism, including photographer. Send the newsletters home to parents.

On page 94 is found a *Make Your Own Puzzles Grid*. This is a page that can be copied over and over again for a variety of purposes. Use it for word search puzzles, crossword puzzles, patterning practice, etc. Give copies to students and, using spelling, vocabulary lists, science, literary, or social studies lists, have them create their own word search or crossword puzzles to exchange with other students. Remind them to create an answer key!

Lastly, *Adding the Equation* on pages 95 and 96 can also be used for a variety of purposes.

My Own Coat of Arms

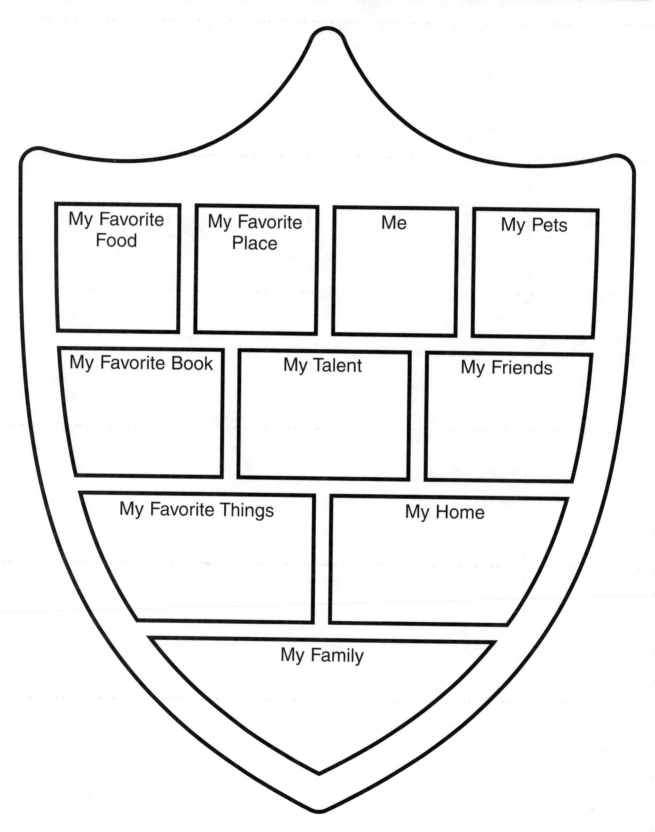

My Favorite Food

My Favorite Place

Me

My Pets

My Favorite Book

My Talent

My Friends

My Favorite Things

My Home

My Family

 **Acrostic Grid**

Alphabet Organizer

Directions: Write a word or a phrase that relates to the topic and begins with each letter.

Topic	A	B	C	D	E	F
G	H	I	J	K	L	M
N	O	P	Q	R	S	T
U	V	W	X	Y	Z	

Imagine What's Missing

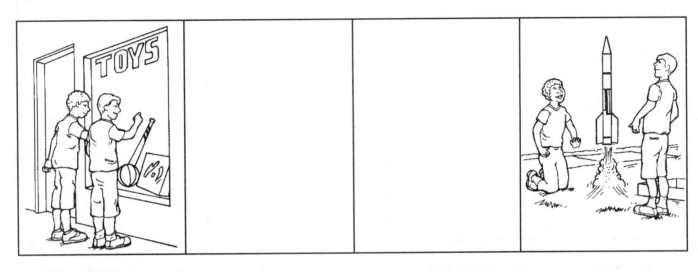

Storyboard

Comic Strip

Creative Tools (Miscellaneous Organizers)

The Newsroom

Directions: Write the news for today. It can be about home, school, family, and friends. Draw pictures to go with the news.

_____ **Daily News**

The Newsroom

Headline:

Byline:	Dateline:
Who?	What?
Where?	Why?
When?	How?

Creative Tools (Miscellaneous Organizers)

Make Your Own Puzzles Grid

_____

(title)

Adding the Equation Example

| Aluminum gets a tough surface film when it reacts with oxygen. | **+** | The film keeps the aluminum from rusting. | **+** | People use aluminum in cars, planes, and buildings because it doesn't rust. | **=** |

Aluminum does not rust when exposed to oxygen.

Adding the Equation

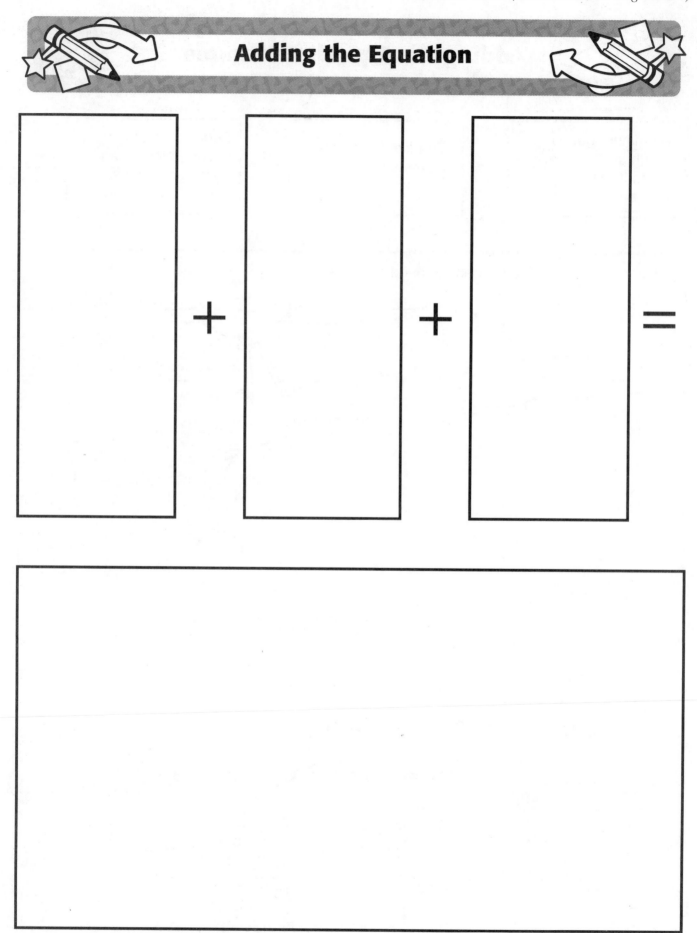